Infill

Development Strategies

Real Estate Research Corporation

Prepared for

U.S. Department of Housing and Urban Development Office of Policy Development and Research Washington, D.C.

Published jointly by
ULI–the Urban Land Institute and
American Planning Association

ULI–the Urban Land Institute is an independent, nonprofit research and educational organization incorporated in 1936 to improve the quality and standards of land use and development. The Institute is committed to conducting practical research in the various fields of real estate knowledge; identifying and interpreting land use trends in relation to the changing economic, social, and civic needs of the people; and disseminating information which can facilitate the orderly and more efficient use and development of land. ULI receives its financial support from membership dues, sale of publications, and contributions for research and panel services.

Ronald R. Rumbaugh
Executive Vice President

The American Planning Association (APA) is the major organization in the country representing the interests of planning and planners. It was formed in 1978 by a merger of the American Institute of Planners and the American Society of Planning Officials. Through its chapters and divisions APA gives members systematic ways to work on problems in common and to affect national planning policies. The American Institute of Certified Planners a part of APA, concentrates on the development of the planning profession, its standards, and continuing education.

Israel Stollman, AICP
Executive Director

ULI Staff

Frank H. Spink, Jr.	Senior Director, Publications
W. Paul O'Mara	Managing Editor
Nadine Huff	Manuscript Editor
Robert L. Helms	Staff Vice President, Operations
Regina P. Agricola	Production Manager
Jeffrey Hughes	Art Director
Betsy Van Buskirk	Artist

Recommended bibliographic listing:
Real Estate Research Corporation. *Infill Development Strategies.*
Washington, D.C.: ULI–the Urban Land Institute and American Planning Association, 1982.

Real Estate Research Corporation Staff for the Infill Study

M. Leanne Lachman, President
Deborah L. Brett, Vice President and Project Manager
Richard E. Starr, Vice President
Cheryl Baxter, Vice President
Robert Miller, Principal Counselor
Sholom Gliksman, Senior Analyst
Joan Papadopoulos, Creative Services Director
Roberta Walker
Linda Hardway
Derrick Southard
Nina Gitz
Charlotte Gore
Linda Mueller
Arlene Nash
Rita Brown
Vicki Gallagher
Patricia McKibben

HUD Government Technical Representative for the Infill Study

James E. Hoben

Table of Contents

For as long as we have seen cities expanding horizontally, less favored parcels of land have been bypassed for development in favor of parcels farther out from a city's core with no physical constraints and suitable for the particular development being proposed. With the advent of rapid suburban development in the 1950s, this development pattern acquired a name—urban sprawl.

Urban sprawl received critical analysis, but for many years little attention was paid to the planning and development of a city's bypassed parcels. Only in central cities where urban renewal activities sought to eliminate blight was attention given to such parcels. Clearance of blighted areas was seen as the strategy for urban revitalization.

A group of emerging forces—rising land prices, rising construction costs, slower approval processes, and a disenchantment with both urban renewal and sprawl, to name a few— occurred at about the same time as the Arab oil embargo and the subsequent rise in energy costs in 1974. The result was a sudden and very dramatic focus on the need to at least consider, if not diligently pursue, the idea of compacting urban areas and reducing the cost of sprawl.

In 1973 the Real Estate Research Corporation (RERC) conducted, under a contract from the Council on Environmental Quality, the Environmental Protection Agency, and the U.S. Department of Housing and Urban Development, a study that ultimately became *The Cost of Sprawl*. It was this study, perhaps more than any other research effort, that induced private and public sector interest in encouraging infill development.

Infill development has and probably should continue to be loosely defined as the process of developing those parcels bypassed during the normal course of urbanization. Understandably, the best and easiest parcels to develop will be first in any cycle of urbanization. What remains after the other parcels are developed are typically those that have problems— difficult soil/drainage or other physical conditions, odd shapes, ownership problems, poor access, land damaged by a pre-urban use (quarries, landfill sites, wrecking yards), or other characteristics. For a long time these problem parcels were ignored or tabled on a community's agenda and not worth the effort for developers who had other options.

But with new interest in infill development, central cities and mature suburban communities have identified infill as a strategy to be examined within their planning and development process. Perhaps even more significantly, developers and builders have begun to be interested in infill development, partly because of the lack of other available sites and partly because they see it as an opportunity for profitable development in a marketplace that now has given greater value to urban proximity.

Despite this interest, little was known about infill land: its magnitude, its characteristics, its potential. Therefore, the U.S. Department of Housing and Urban Development (HUD) commissioned RERC, which had done the earlier study of the cost of sprawl, to undertake a comprehensive analysis of infill opportunities and constraints.

While it was recognized that each community probably had its own characteristics with regard to bypassed land available for infill development, it was also felt that carefully selected detailed case studies covering an entire metropolitan area would provide resonably universal strategies for and conclusions about infill development. The study focused on three diverse metropolitan counties—Miami, Florida (Dade County); Seattle, Washington (King County); and Rochester, New York (Monroe County). Approximately 500 parcels were examined in terms of their size, ownership, zoning, physical characteristics, availability for development, neighborhood dynamics, and marketability. A comparative study was also made of development costs on infill sites at the urban fringe. Although generalizations about national potential certainly cannot be made on the basis of only three in-depth case studies, especially for a phenomenon as multifaceted as infill development, there are commonalities which emerged in each of the three metropolitan areas that can provide guidance for cities and developers alike in understanding and pursuing a strategy of infill development.

While RERC's final report to HUD was organized differently than the format of this book, the format presented here is intended to provide access to the results of the research effort in the most useful way for a variety of audiences. Therefore the publication is divided into two parts.

Part I is a guide for local officials and developers carrying out infill programs. The examples of programs that have been implemented or are under consideration are intended both as illustrations and as sources for further information. Chapter 1 synthesizes the research findings on infill opportunities and constraints. Chapter 2 examines information needed to formulate an infill strategy at the regional, municipal, or neighborhood level. It also suggests ways in which cities can share information on infill development opportunities with the private building industry and with citizen groups. Chapter 3 looks at tools and incentives for encouraging investment on bypassed sites by removing regulatory obstacles, reducing risk, upgrading infrastructure, lowering land costs, or otherwise helping to make infill development competitive with expansion at the suburban fringe. The focus is on expanding housing opportunities, although many of the techniques can also be used for commercial or industrial development.

Part II examines RERC's research findings in more detail. Chapter 4 looks at the quantity of infill land in each of the three case study counties, comparing the residential infill land supply with the demand for new housing over the next 10 years. Chapter 5 examines key characteristics of individual infill parcels from the perspective of the developer/builder— their size, location, zoning, physical limitations, ownership, and availability. The nature and extent of those deterrents to infilling most frequently cited by real estate interests are reviewed. Cost comparisons of infill and fringe development in the three metropolitan areas are presented in Chapter 6.

ULI's and APA's role in encouraging infill development through publication of this book is based on the idea that it is an effective method of filling the holes in the urban fabric provided that there is conscious encouragement on the part of the community and by developers who are willing to participate in what can be good development opportunities.

Frank H. Spink, Jr.
Senior Director of Publications
ULI—the Urban Land Institute

Frank S. So, AICP
Deputy Executive Director
American Planning Association

Part I

Infill Development Potential

Vacant, skipped-over parcels of land in otherwise built-up areas can be identified in every city. These "infill" sites can result from a lack of or access to public services, physical/environmental limitations, or a general unattractiveness to the market. Encouraging development of such parcels has become an objective for federal, state, and local governments faced with, among other things, rising energy costs, a decreasing capability to expand infrastructure at the urban fringe, pressures to preserve environmentally sensitive or agricultural land, the need to strengthen older neighborhoods through preservation and rehabilitation, and an interest in improving transit accessibility.

Infill development is becoming increasingly popular as a response to some of the current and future concerns of our cities. It can be a means of protecting and enhancing as well as revitalizing older neighborhoods. It is also a way of saving energy through greater use of attached housing and through better employment/residence proximity. Congressional hearings on the subject concluded that "urban flight in recent decades has left large amounts of unused infrastructure in center cities, close-in suburbs, and small towns. This excess capacity offers opportunities for compactness and energy saving in the 1980s for communities across the nation."[1]

Concern about escalating housing costs has also prompted renewed interest in infill development as a way of containing the rate of future price increases. In theory, building on skipped-over land with full services already in place should be less costly than using land at the fringe, which must be provided with on-site roads and utilities, and where developers are now required to make land or fee donations to cover school and park costs. The Council on Development Choices for the '80s, a panel of 37 leaders in governmental affairs, development, finance, and the design professions, recommended infill development, along with other compact development techniques, as a means of keeping down the costs of housing and energy.

Infill development is also seen as a method of preserving land while accommodating growth. Concern has been expressed at all levels of government over the continued loss of productive farmland as urbanization spreads.

A 1974 Department of Agriculture study indicated that 750,000 acres of cropland were lost each year, of which perhaps 300,000 were actively employed in crop production.[2] Much higher losses were cited in the controversial National Agricultural Lands Study,[3] sponsored by the U.S. Department of Agriculture and the Council on Environmental Quality. That report estimated that a total of three million acres were shifted annually from agricultural to nonagricultural use between 1968 and 1975. Just under one million acres per year were in farms or cropland, of which 600,000 were converted to urban or transportation use. Cropland loss to urban uses is irreversible.

It has been estimated that more than 40 percent of the housing built in the 1970s was constructed on rural land outside of Standard Metropolitan Statistical Areas (SMSAs). The likelihood of development pressures affecting prime cropland increases closer to major metropolitan areas. Flat, well-drained acreage with good soil conditions is attractive to developers and farmers. Even though per-acre yields are increasing on remaining productive farmland and newly productive acreage is being created, concerns are voiced about the ability of U.S. agriculture to continue to provide its share of rising world food needs at reasonable prices. Land at the urban fringe (especially in growing southern California cities) is often among the most productive for agricultural use.

State land use policies are also being targeted toward agricultural land preservation. Oregon has mandated exclusive agricultural use zoning and the creation of transition areas (buffers) of open space that separate urban from agricultural lands. In addition, public services that pass through agricultural lands cannot be hooked up to nonfarm uses.[4]

A HUD-sponsored analysis of state urban strategies found that "the states' focus on growth management concentrated on twin objectives: controlling urban sprawl and protecting environmentally sensitive areas. The antisprawl measures were essentially a combination of

---

[1] U.S. House of Representatives, Committee on Banking, Finance and Urban Affairs, Subcommittee on the City, *Compact Cities: Energy Saving Strategies For the Eighties* (Washington, D.C.: U.S. Government Printing Office, July 1980) p. 14. For a complete review of the arguments for infill as an energy saving development technique, see Corbin Crews Harwood, *Using Land To Save Energy* (Cambridge: Ballinger Publishing Company, 1977).

[2] *The President's National Urban Policy Report: 1980*, Prepared by the U.S. Department of Housing and Urban Development. (HUD-583-1-CPD), pp. 9–18.

[3] U.S. Department of Agriculture and Council on Environmental Quality, *National Agricultural Lands Study*, Final Report (Washington, D.C.: GPO, 1981), pp. 13, 25.

[4] State of Oregon, Land Conservation and Development Commission, *Statewide Planning Goals and Guidelines* (September 1978).

Agricultural land for sale in Monroe County, New York.

infilling and agricultural preservation policies."[5] Goal #4 of the 1978 California Urban Strategy refers to "curbing wasteful urban sprawl *and* directing new development to existing cities and suburbs."[6] Some states have concentrated on natural resource protection issues as a means of encouraging infill development. This is especially true of Florida and Washington, where state laws mandate careful environmental impact review of private development projects, as well as public projects such as highways or sewer lines.

Tempering Infill Expectations

Despite the widespread public interest in infill development, some cautions should be cited about specific expectations. Using land that already has public services can reduce government capital expenditures. But whether the existing infrastructure is a real asset that can be used to attract developers to infill locations depends on how well it has been maintained and whether it meets today's design standards. Many older neighborhoods will need upgraded infrastructure, whether or not they develop infill parcels. In an era of fiscal restraints, it will be difficult for local governments to raise the funds needed to continue current maintenance levels and correct past problems. New infill projects will, however, help to distribute the cost burden among a larger number of users.

Surplus water and sewer capacity exists in older cities where populations have declined and in newer suburbs where systems were oversized. The cost of maintenance must be spread among a smaller number of users than is desirable. City finance officials voice eagerness to attract new development on already serviced parcels to help share the costs of a relatively fixed maintenance and operations burden.

At the urban fringe, the growing "taxpayer revolt" means that bond issues for new facilities (and the taxes to maintain them) are being increasingly rejected by the voters. Nearly 80 percent of all bond issues were approved in the 1950s, but only 53 percent gained approval between 1971 and 1978.[7] In part a reaction to higher tax burdens, rejection of bond issues also reflects an unwillingness to support public facilities that will induce changes in community character—a loss of small town atmosphere or a fear of urbanization. Tax limitations, such as those posed by Proposition 13 in California and Proposition 2½ in Massachusetts, also make it difficult for cities to issue bonds and still fund ongoing services. Even where bond issues are being approved, jurisdictions find that increasing competition for capital is driving up interest rates on municipal bonds beyond what is considered acceptable under state laws and local policies.

Existing water and sewer systems, schools, libraries, and road networks can offer major attractions to builders seeking ways to reduce front-end capital investment or the delays that are inevitable when waiting for governments to extend services in an uncertain fiscal climate. Recent studies indicate, however, that many cities are falling far behind in routine maintenance and replacement of their aging infrastructure systems. As budgets are cut back, capital outlay is curtailed and maintenance staffs are reduced. Some cities have been able to substitute new labor-saving equipment to meet this challenge, but others have not. A study of 28 cities conducted by the Urban Institute suggests that maintenance practices and resulting conditions vary widely from city to city. For example, resurfacing of major streets was found to be behind schedule for 90 percent of the system in Newark, 50 percent in Cincinnati, and 25 percent in Dallas.[8]

[5] Charles R. Warren, *The States and Urban Strategies: A Comparative Analysis*, prepared by the National Academy of Public Administration for the Office Of Policy Development and Research, U.S. Department of Housing and Urban Development (September 1980), p. 29.

[6] State of California, *An Urban Strategy for California* (Sacramento: Office of Planning and Research, 1978).

[7] Rochelle L. Stanfield, "Building Streets and Sewers is Easy—It's Keeping Them Up That's The Trick," *National Journal*, May 24, 1980, p. 845.

[8] Nan Humphrey and Peter Wilson, "Capital Stock Condition in 28 Cities", unpublished paper by Urban Institute, October 1, 1979. See also *America's Urban Capital Stock*, an Urban Institute series edited by George E. Peterson focusing on conditions in New York City, Cleveland, Cincinnati, Dallas, Boston, and Oakland.

That older urban communities have strong needs for increased investment in their capital stock and for improvement in ongoing services has been documented. However, these expenditures are required not just to attract a few new construction projects on infill lots but also to provide better service to persons and businesses located in these urbanized areas.

Preserving Agricultural Land at the Urban Fringe

Not all regions have extensive preservicing of fringe area land in anticipation of development. To limit escalation in raw land prices and housing costs, it may be necessary to allow further extension or urban services and utilities. At least some industrial users will look to the urban fringe for future sites because sufficiently large vacant tracts usually do not exist in already built-up areas—at least not without demolishing existing structures.

Sensitive growth management recognizes these limitations to infilling. For example, more than half the vacant acreage within King County, Washington's, sewerage planning area is not fully served with both water and sewer. Service extensions are generally permitted within this vast unserved area.

Rural land will become urbanized in the next decade in both metropolitan and nonmetropolitan areas, but the pace of conversion need not proceed at the same rate as over the last two decades. Recognition of infill development potential, combined with prudent use of development controls at the urban fringe, can result in protecting thousands of agricultural acres in the next 10 years.

Reducing Land Costs

Land costs are a growing component of residential and nonresidential development costs. Asking prices for the remaining vacant parcels in attractive infill neighborhoods reflect the stability of these areas and their proximity to jobs, schools, shopping, and transportation. Builders and realtors interviewed as part of the case studies and in other related research consistently cite high urban land prices as a major deterrent to the financial feasibility of infill construction when compared with fringe development.[9]

The high cost of infill land may be offset if local governments allow higher density development than is typically permitted at the urban fringe. Minimum per-unit lot areas are usually smaller in central cities than in the outlying suburbs, but the differences are often not enough to offset the higher city land costs. Because land prices in attractive infill locations are high, developers will seek rezoning or variances that will allow more economical use of a site. This keeps per-unit costs lower and hence broadens the affordability of housing built on the site.

The Council on Development Choices for the '80s recently urged that local government permit and encourage increased overall densities by reducing requirements for lot and yard sizes, setbacks, and street widths, and by assuring adequate amounts of land zoned for varying densities. This would allow freedom of choice for housing consumers while at the same time avoiding undue cost increases. The Council believes that greater compactness of development can be achieved through selective increases in density while retaining the character and attractiveness of single-family neighborhoods.[10]

Conserving Energy

The 1980 *National Urban Policy Report* cautioned that use of smaller cars and greater reliance on multifamily dwelling units (with shared-wall construction and small floor areas) would conserve energy more effectively than would more compact development patterns.[11] As households reduce auto usage and as employment opportunities decentralize, channeling housing construction to close-in, passed-over lands may not cause dramatic further reductions in the journey to work.

Supporting Existing Neighborhoods

Infill development might strengthen older city and suburban neighborhoods by bringing in new capital investment. However, existing residents and businesses may not always view infilling as advantageous for them.

---

9 One example can be found in results of interviews conducted by the city of Omaha Planning Department. See "Urban Infill Interviews: Overview Comments and Suggestions from the Omaha Development Community" unpublished paper, 1980.

10 See *The Affordable Community: Adapting Today's Communities to Tomorrow's Needs* (Washington, D.C.: ULI–the Urban Land Institute, 1982).

11 *The President's National Urban Policy Report: 1980* (HUD-583-1-CPD), pp. 9–15.

Where vacant land exists in stabilized neighborhoods, sensitive infilling should be seen as a logical extension of successful neighborhood preservation. Industrial infilling can provide needed jobs close to where available workers live. New housing will appeal to the middle-income taxpayers whom cities want to attract and retain, while at the same time increasing the population base that supports neighborhood retailing and cultural institutions. Infilling also eliminates vacant lots that can become an eyesore when not properly maintained. By indicating private sector confidence in a neighborhood's future, new infill development can also stimulate further investment in residential and commercial rehabilitation.

There is a good deal of developer interest in vacant lots that remain in the most attractive locations. Yet there are very few investors who are willing to be pioneers in low-income neighborhoods that have deteriorated housing or weak commercial strips. They will wait for the existing building stock to be upgraded and for values of existing properties to rise before risking new construction projects.

The amount of acreage potentially available for infill development is not very extensive in most middle- or upper-income neighborhoods. Furthermore, residents are often eager to preserve what little "open space" may exist. In locations with historic character and scale, homeowners are concerned that infill development will not be compatible with existing building styles and scale.

Cities which want to encourage infill will have to anticipate conflicts between builders and local interest groups. A common neighborhood complaint is the design compatibility of new buildings with surrounding structures.

In Seattle, for example, building height and bulk are concerns to those who currently enjoy attractive views of Puget Sound or Lake Washington and who have paid premium prices for these amenities. Opposition to infilling can also focus on traffic and parking problems that would be exacerbated by additional people or businesses. In low-income neighborhoods, residents may view infilling as the beginning of gentrification and displacement, depending on the type of development proposed. For other projects, opposition will be couched in economic terms—the effects of scattered-site Section 8 housing on surrounding property values or of new commercial space in an area with existing vacant storefronts or offices.

Concern about neighborhood opposition to infilling was echoed by builders interviewed by the city of Omaha officials who listed neighborhood resistance as one of the five most important problems limiting their ability to develop infill housing. It is important, though, not to exaggerate the influence of neighborhood groups in curtailing infill development potential. The majority of infill projects are probably not controversial and most seem to move through the approval process with little difficulty. Where objections are raised, they are often legitimate.

City governments that want to encourage infill development will have to anticipate, plan for, and resolve conflicts between builders and local interest groups. One of the most common neighborhood concerns is the compatibility of new building design with the surrounding structures. Sensitive design solutions are often possible—using similar facades and setbacks, for example. However, if the initial proposal is for an incompatible structure, nearby property owners may be righteously indignant and force expensive and unpleasant confrontations.

Residents and local business owners may be extremely aware of aging sewer and water systems that lack the capacity to handle additional loads or to withstand the jarring of heavy construction. Again, opposition can be reduced if the city and developer will address these problems first.

Many developers who are accustomed to building at the urban fringe are extremely apprehensive about neighborhood protests. Thus, they look to local government for help in obtaining approvals and mitigating neighborhood opposition.

Infill Land Characteristics

Although interest in infill development was emerging, little was known about the magnitude, characteristics, or development potential of these vacant sites. Some of the questions raised were:

- How much vacant land exists in already urbanized portions of metropolitan areas? Are infill opportunities largely urban or suburban?
- How much of this supply is free of physical or environmental constraints to development?
- Is the supply of infill land well located with respect to market demand?
- Who owns infill land? Will the owners make it available for development now or in the near future?
- How much of the demand for developable land can be satisfied through infilling? How does this differ among regions of varying sizes and growth rates?
- What are the relative costs of developing infill land and building at the urban fringe? Do transportation cost savings for property users cancel out the higher per-square-foot costs of closer-in land?

Recognizing this lack of information, the U.S. Department of Housing and Urban Development commissioned Real Estate Research Corporation (RERC) to undertake a comprehensive analysis of infill opportunities and constraints. Their primary focus was on detailed case studies of infill parcels and their development potential in three diverse metropolitan counties—Miami, Florida (Dade County); Seattle, Washington (King County); and Rochester, New York (Monroe County). In all, approximately 500 parcels were examined in terms of their size, ownership, zoning, physical characteristics, availability for development, neighborhood dynamics, and marketability. Although generalizations about national potential certainly cannot be made on the basis of three in-depth case studies, especially for a phenomenon as multifaceted as infill, commonalities emerged in the three metropolitan areas that provide guidance for cities and developers alike.

Looking at the results of the three case studies, vacant infill land represented 37,000 acres in urbanized Miami (Dade County); 70,000 acres in Seattle (King County); and 66,000 acres in Rochester (Monroe County). After eliminating nonresidential sites, property currently unavailable for development, and parcels with physical or market limitations, RERC found that there were approximately 10,000 acres of residential infill land in

Miami; 24,000 acres in Seattle; and 13,000 acres in Rochester. These properties could theoretically accommodate two-thirds of Miami's, nearly all of Seattle's, and all of Rochester's residential growth for the next 10 years. (For a more detailed discussion of these research findings see Part II.)

It would not be advisable, however, to force all future growth onto these sites because there is also a market need for development at the urban fringe. Infill development should not be viewed as a panacea that will accommodate all future growth. Infill potential can vary significantly among metropolitan areas, as suggested in Figure 1-1. Building will continue at the urban fringe, but at a slower pace than in the 1950s, 1960s, and 1970s. Rehabilitation and redevelopment of underutilized lands should also capture a significant share of development demand. Certain infill tracts should probably remain vacant in areas with critical shortages of open space. To avoid unacceptable inflation of land prices, the market must remain competitive in terms of locational choice and quantity of supply.

Parcel Sizes and Assembly Potential

Infill parcels ranged from less than ¼ acre to 20 acres or more. As shown in Figure 1-2, there were relatively few individual parcels with more than five acres. Over half the lots in all three areas were ¼ acre or less—the equivalent of the average single-family detached homesite. The size patterns were similar from city to city, but there were a greater number of smaller parcels in the Miami area, which has the strongest and highest value real estate market of the three. Clearly, intense development pressure on the larger parcels that existed five or 10 years ago had already been felt.

The capacity of small infill parcels to meet market demand may be substantially enhanced by land assembly. In Seattle and Rochester, between 50 percent and 60 percent of the sampled infill parcels were observed to be adjacent to other vacant land. In Miami, infill sites were slightly more isolated, with only 40 percent bordered by another undeveloped property. Most of this land was not in single ownership. RERC staff also found numerous instances where infill parcels abutted underutilized properties that could be redeveloped in conjunction with a project on the vacant site next door. Consolidating infill parcels into larger, more easily developable sites

Figure 1-1
Factors Affecting Infill Potential

Factors	Highest Potential	Lowest Potential
Growth	Rapidly growing population; extensive demand for new housing	No population growth; limited new household formation
Employment Centers	Strong CBD and local employment nodes; long commuting distances from the urban fringe	Weak CBD; dispersed employment centers; short commutes from the fringe to jobs
Building Conditions	Extensive investment (public and private) in neighborhood preservation and upgrading	Little investment in existing building stock or public facilities
Resident Incomes	Infill land located in a variety of neighborhoods serving many income groups	Infill land concentrated in low-income neighborhoods
Land Prices	Shallow land price gradient from urban fringe to inner city or significant density differences to balance steep gradient	Steep land price gradient from urban fringe to inner city and little variation in land use densities
Growth Controls	Limits on outward spread of development operating region-wide	No growth guidance or coordination among jurisdictions
Availability And Cost Of Services	Developers at the fringe pay costs of service extensions and assist with school and park requirements; limited preservicing	Extensive preservicing; little in the way of impact fees charged

Figure 1-2
Size Distribution of Sampled Infill Tax Parcels
Three Case Studies

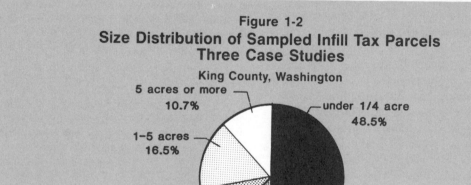

King County, Washington

5 acres or more 10.7%
1-5 acres 16.5%
1/2-1 acre 8.9%
1/4-1/2 acre 15.4%
under 1/4 acre 48.5%

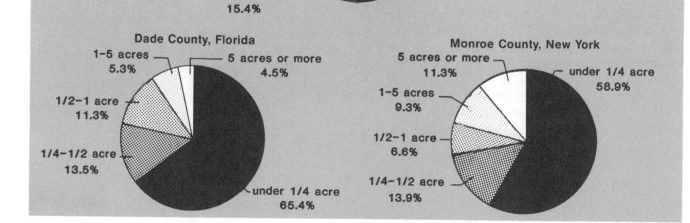

Dade County, Florida

1-5 acres 5.3%
5 acres or more 4.5%
1/2-1 acre 11.3%
1/4-1/2 acre 13.5%
under 1/4 acre 65.4%

Monroe County, New York

5 acres or more 11.3%
under 1/4 acre 58.9%
1-5 acres 9.3%
1/2-1 acre 6.6%
1/4-1/2 acre 13.9%

will, in most cases, call for coordinated land assembly involving multiple owners. This adds to the complexity of development but may increase the rewards as well.

Physical Attributes

The vast majority of infill sites studied were free of severe physical limitations to development. Certain vacant sites—such as remnants from highway construction or long but narrow abandoned rights-of-way—would be difficult to develop, if at all. Other limitations, such as steep slopes or flood-prone locations, could be corrected through careful design. Specialized construction techniques enhance the attractiveness of difficult-to-develop parcels that were skipped over years ago. However, sensitive sites cannot be developed at the same densities that are possible for unconstrained land; per-unit construction costs can be high.

Infrastructure Conditions

Although infill sites, by definition, have access to roads, utilities, and other public services, their condition or capacity is not always adequate to support new development—especially large-scale, high-density projects. For example, 15 percent of the sampled infill parcels in urbanized King County lacked direct frontage on public roads. In Dade County, one-third of the sites had public water lines with diameters smaller than the standard six inches needed to maintain adequate pressure and fire flow for development at urban densities. It was not uncommon to find water and sewer lines that were over 50 years old serving infill parcels.

Maintenance practices varied considerably among jurisdictions. Fiscal limitations, especially in older central cities, can result in deferred spending on capital upgrading and replacement. These problems need public attention, not only to encourage infilling but also to stimulate and to reinforce investment in existing buildings in older neighborhoods.

Zoning

In all metropolitan areas, some degree of "mismatch" exists between market demand and the zoning designations of the vacant land supply. Communities "overzone" for industrial or commercial uses in the hope of attracting tax ratables. Not enough land is designated for multi-family housing, which can make efficient use of expensive infill sites.

Of the owners of available infill properties interviewed as part of this study, roughly 25 percent in all three cases felt that some change in existing zoning would improve the marketability of their land. In a rapidly changing real estate market, it is impossible to achieve a perfect balance between zoning and the demand for land. Community preferences must also be considered. Nevertheless, inappropriate zoning can be a deterrent to infilling. In weak markets, downzoning has been suggested as a way of reducing artificially high land prices. In desirable areas, density bonuses may be needed to make development more economical.

Location of Infill Lots

In all three urban counties examined, a majority of infill lots were located in the suburbs. Lots in Miami/Miami Beach accounted for only 28 percent of all infill parcels; for Seattle, the central city share was 41 percent. Lots in the city of Rochester were somewhat more numerous, accounting for 47 percent of the total. City lots in Miami and Rochester were often clustered in low-income neighborhoods, thereby limiting their marketability.

More important was the considerable size disparity between infill parcels in central cities and those in the suburbs. Suburban sites were far larger, as shown in Figure 1-3. As a result, they accounted for over 90 percent of the infill acreage in all three cases. Central cities that annexed undeveloped areas during the era of suburbanization are more likely to contain large vacant tracts within their corporate limits. If unconstrained by zoning or physical limitations, these tracts will be more readily marketable.

An inner-city lot awaiting development.

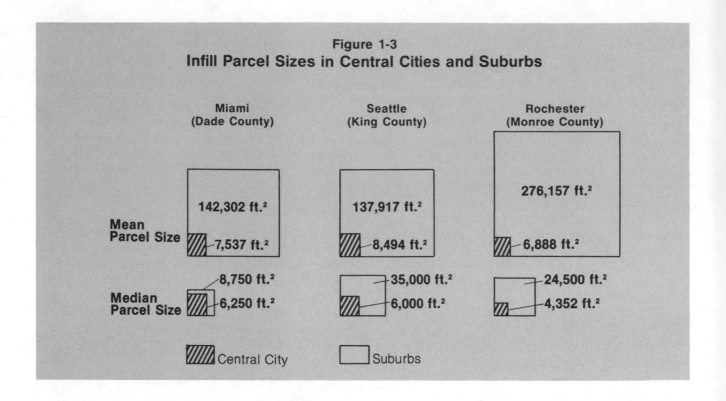

Figure 1-3
Infill Parcel Sizes in Central Cities and Suburbs

| Miami (Dade County) | Seattle (King County) | Rochester (Monroe County) |

Mean Parcel Size
Miami: 142,302 ft.² — 7,537 ft.²
Seattle: 137,917 ft.² — 8,494 ft.²
Rochester: 276,157 ft.² — 6,888 ft.²

Median Parcel Size
Miami: 8,750 ft.² — 6,250 ft.²
Seattle: 35,000 ft.² — 6,000 ft.²
Rochester: 24,500 ft.² — 4,352 ft.²

Central City   Suburbs

Land Ownership

Infill land is owned by many entities. In all three metropolitan areas, as illustrated in Figure 1-4, more than half of the sample parcels were held by individuals. Businesses controlled far fewer of the vacant parcels than many observers would expect. Government owners were overrepresented in the Monroe County sample because many vacant properties there were tax delinquent or were cleared years ago by the Rochester Urban Renewal Authority. If government properties are excluded from the inventories, the proportion of parcels in individual (as opposed to business) ownership was 63 percent in Dade County, 69 percent in Monroe County, and 71 percent in the Seattle area. This means that of privately held sites, about two-thirds were controlled by individuals.

Only one-fourth of the infill parcels examined in RERC's investigation were owned by people who were engaged primarily in the real estate business. Speculators who purposely hold property off the market are not the dominant holders of vacant urban land. Major corporations or institutions can control larger properties that are most attractive to the typical big suburban builders, although this was not true of the three case study areas.

The vast majority of infill parcels were owned by individuals and businesses located within the metropolitan area, not foreigners or corporations located in another part of the country. Ownership by outsiders accounted for less than one-fifth of all parcels examined.

Land Availability

Not all of the infill land supply is available for development. In fact, just over half of the approximately 500 parcels surveyed were on the market or would be within five years. Availability of land was highest in Rochester (62 percent), whereas in Seattle and Miami, the figures were 50 percent and 53 percent, respectively. The real estate knowledge and sophistication of infill land owners varied considerably. However, owners of sites who would make their properties available for development voiced strong optimism about future development potential. As indicated in Figure 1-5, fully half to three-fourths of infill site owners believe that the market for

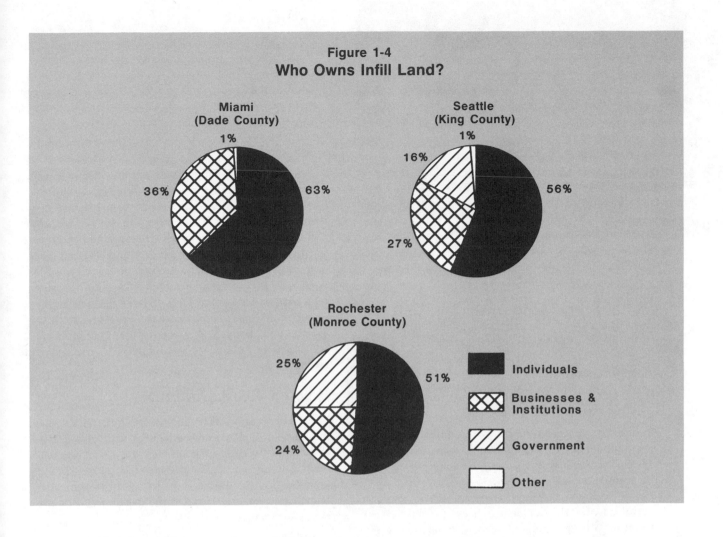

Figure 1-4
Who Owns Infill Land?

Miami
(Dade County)

1%
36%
63%

Seattle
(King County)

1%
16%
27%
56%

Rochester
(Monroe County)

25%
24%
51%

■ Individuals
▨ Businesses & Institutions
▨ Government
□ Other

Figure 1-5
Owners' Assessment of Change in the Market for Infill Land, Next Five Years

	Miami (Dade County)	Seattle (King County)	Rochester (Monroe County)
Will Improve	82%	74%	49%
Will Stay the Same	16%	9%	34%
Will Weaken	0%	8%	0%
Not Sure	2%	9%	18%

Just over half of the nearly 500 infill parcels surveyed by Real Estate Research Corporation were on the market or would be in five years.

their land would improve over the next five years. This may help to explain the fact that only half of all privately owned infill sites were available for purchase or lease.

Owner Motives

RERC's research suggests that there are three dominant reasons for owners holding vacant land:

- *Future appreciation/investment*—the primary motivating force for both individuals and businesses.
- *Personal use*—most significant for vacant parcels adjacent to existing residences.
- *Future expansion*—providing reserves for both business and residential development. This is also the motivation for government agencies' retention of land for anticipated facility needs, though some of those needs may no longer exist in cities with stable or declining populations.

The properties being held for appreciation or investment, and some of those reserved for expansion, could be made available for development, given positive market conditions, workable financing, and the right price. Overall, about half the parcels examined could be deemed available.

Land Prices and Housing Costs

Infill land in stable, middle-income neighborhoods can be as much as 12 times as expensive, on an average per-unit basis, than raw land at the metropolitan fringe. As seen in Figure 1-6, new infrastructure costs can be significantly less for infill housing than for identical units at the suburban fringe, but the savings will usually be insufficient to offset higher land prices in stable, mature neighborhoods. Small infill parcels that can make maximum use of existing in-place utilities will have minimal site improvement costs. Larger infill projects require creation of on-site roads and utilities. Costs per dwelling unit for larger infill sites will not be dramatically lower than for development at the urban fringe.

High land prices, per se, will not necessarily limit development. The key factor is what can be built and sold or rented on the land and the relationship between sales prices or rental rates and land cost. In other words, the developer will pay high land prices if the final package of land and building will command high rents or a high sales price.

For housing consumers, trade-offs are evident between central city and fringe locations when commuting and total transportation costs are taken into account, as shown in Figure 1-7. For example, an average household living at the urban fringe in Rochester could be expected to spend $3,100 more per year on commuting and auto ownership than the same household in the city of Rochester. In metropolitan Miami, the contrasts were even sharper. A western Dade County resident might spend $4,000 more annually than one in the Little Havana neighborhood of Miami. This equation is being considered by more and more households as energy costs escalate.

Role for Local Government

As interest in infill heightens, local public agencies should take steps to become familiar with, to identify, and to classify vacant parcels within their jurisdictions. A number of cities and counties are examining infill potential and limitations, but most local governments remain only vaguely aware of the location and extent of skipped-over properties.

To become more familiar with the amount of vacant land, cities can prepare inventories and market analyses for available sites, particularly those that fit the general description in Figure 1-8, and then distribute the information to local real estate brokers and developers.

An interim use for a vacant parcel in the Rochester area.

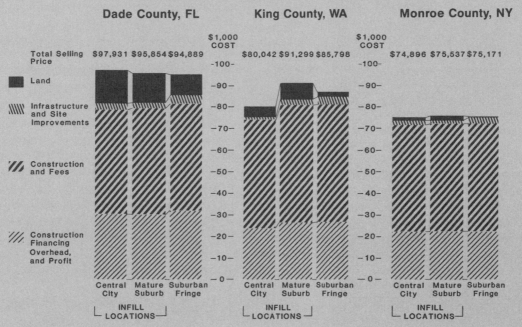

Figure 1-6
Comparison of Development Costs Components for Townhouses in Three Locations
(Weighted Average Per-Unit Costs)

Figure 1-7
Comparison of Average Annual Transportation Costs in Case Study Locations

Infill Locations	Miami (Dade County)	Seattle (King County)	Rochester (Monroe County)
Central City	$1,298	$2,210	$2,539
Mature Suburb	3,031	4,111	3,802
Suburban Fringe	5,338	6,219	5,598

Figure 1-8
The Optimum Infill Site

The Context
- Viable market area
- Compatible, well-maintained surrounding properties
- Receptive neighborhood
- Helpful city government
- Absence of environmental problems
- Workable building code
- Good public services

The Property
- For sale at realistic price
- Sufficient size for intended use
- Perceived market for intended use(s)
- Adequate utilities in place
- Street frontage
- Regularly shaped developable parcels
- No major topographic, drainage, or subsoil problem
- Appropriate zoning
- Potential development profitability comparable to alternative sites

Local agencies also play an important role in determining project feasibility, mainly through traditional activities, such as zoning and planning reviews, and by capital investment programs to build roads, sewers, and water mains. Techniques that can be used to encourage infill range from passive efforts at technical assistance (for both developers and neighborhood groups) to modified codes and review procedures or more conscious targeting of capital improvements. Creative liaison with neighborhood groups that oppose new construction projects is emerging as a legitimate public activity. Other techniques being used to encourage rehabilitation and redevelopment—such as tax abatement or tax increment financing—can also be used to assist infill projects.

These and other techniques that have been used in specific localities and are suitable for encouragement of infill are listed in Figure 1-9. The list is representative, rather than comprehensive, and few of the techniques are unique to infill usage. Most of them are familiar to city planners and building officials, but they may not have been targeted as yet to this application.

Efficient processing can go a long way in allaying developers' fears and creating a positive environment for infill development. This is particularly important given the fact that most infill parcels are small and therefore appeal to the small- or medium-sized developer. Such individuals and companies typically have limited staff time and are relatively inexperienced in dealing with a wide range of government agencies. Because time is money in development, expediting permit processing is essential to generating widespread developer interest in infill.

Reconciling the competing concerns of private developers, neighboring property owners, and local governments is not an easy task. But there is ample evidence that it can work, and that market conditions are now more favorable for infilling than they have been in the last 20 years. Opportunities are available for the private sector to make a profit while acting in concert with public goals for sound urban development.

Figure 1-9
Tools and Techniques for Encouraging Infilling

Needed Actions	Possible Incentives	Target Opportunities	Cautions
Stimulating Developer Interest in Infilling	Training programs/seminars/publicity campaign	Outreach to builders, developers, and realtors through professional associations and the news media	May have to go outside the region for speakers who have had success with infilling
	Parcel files; information on prototype projects	Comprehensive; or only for special uses (multifamily; industrial)	Needs careful staff supervision
	Design competitions	For scattered small lots; for large areas offering unique opportunities	Needs volunteers to serve on review committees and needs funds for prizes
Removing Obstacles Created by Government			
Reducing delays in project review	Reform of staff review procedures	Small-scale projects	Must assure adequate citizen participation
	Elimination of unnecessary hearings	Projects requiring variances or special use permits	Requires cooperation of many city departments and staff members

	Creation of ombudsman or expeditor	All projects; or just those involving assisted housing or employment generation	Obstacles in state enabling legislation
Correcting excessively high or inappropriate standards	Reexamination of code provisions; encouragement of performance-based requirements	All infill projects; could also be important in redevelopment and rehabilitation	May encounter resistance from city staff, building trades, or neighborhood groups; results will not be immediately visible
Improving zoning balance (not enough multifamily land; overzoning for industrial use)	Comprehensive review of zoning map and/or regulations	Citywide or in designated neighborhoods as part of the neighborhood planning process	May encounter resistance from neighborhood residents and property owners depending on the types of changes proposed. Must be based on sound market analysis
Creating Neighborhood Support for Infilling	Inclusion in neighborhood plans of strategies for dealing with vacant lots	All neighborhoods (especially those with high potential)	Neighbors must see advantages for existing housing and businesses as well as the developer if they are to be convinced; developers must be flexible and willing to listen
	Project review meetings with developer in advance of official hearings	All projects likely to generate controversy	May also need to meet neighborhood groups in advance
Addressing Market Weakness or Uncertainty/Poor Area Image	Demonstration projects involving local development corporations and neighborhood interests	Low- and moderate-income neighborhoods, especially for projects providing jobs and/or increased shopping or services	Builds confidence if successful; high risk; limited expertise in dealing with risky situations
	Loan guarantees	Projects in areas with poor image but location advantages (i.e., near jobs, transit, major institutions)	Risk of unsuccessful projects requires expertise of experienced builders and banks
	"Below-market" financing through mortgage revenue bonds or industrial bond programs	Target neighborhoods and projects where special financing terms can act as a "magnet" to households or businesses who would otherwise locate at the urban fringe	Recent federal legislative limitations; need for careful market studies

	Greater attention to maintenance and rehabilitation	Low- and moderate-income neighborhoods	Concern over long-term displacement of the poor
	Visible public commitment to upgrading public works	Target neighborhoods	Resistance to targeting on a neighborhood basis
	Interim uses (parking, gardens, play areas)	Areas with established neighborhood organizations that will assume maintenance responsibility; areas with open space or parking needs	High maintenance burdens; resistance to future change

Addressing Site-Specific Problems

Reducing the high cost of infill land	Land price write-down	Unique opportunity to achieve public purpose	High costs if used extensively; adverse political impacts from using public funds to subsidize strictly private projects
	Tax abatement	Definite project with committed developer	
	Leasing of publicly owned land	Varies; generally used for housing developments priced for low/moderate-income occupancy	Careful lease structuring needed to protect public interest
	Density bonuses; permitting variances from side-yards or setbacks to allow greater coverage	Mixed-use projects; projects incorporating assisted housing	Need to assure design compatibility with surrounding areas; possible opposition of neighbors
	Forgiveness of delinquent back taxes	Definite projects with committed developers	Legal obstacles in some states
	Downzoning	Areas where permitted densities do not match local housing market preferences	Objections of landowners
	Fee waivers	All infill projects	Fees are not a high proportion of project costs; effects are more psychological than financial

Increasing land availability	Property tax "disincentives" —site value taxation —higher taxes on vacant land	Vacant land in marketable locations (targeting will be difficult if not impossible)	Adverse effects on vacant property owners in deteriorated areas; adverse effects on existing buildings in "hot" neighborhoods
	Land assembly (vacant land only or vacant and underutilized sites)	Definite projects with committed developers	Expensive; legal limitations on use of eminent domain powers
	Land banking	Areas with extensive scattered parcels; high incidence of tax delinquency	Expensive; may require enabling legislation; land may not be marketable in the short run, especially in weak markets
Correcting infrastructure problems	Public funding of off-site capital improvements (minor street and utility extensions or upgrading)	Small-scale infilling, especially for industrial use	Reluctance of elected officials to target limited CIP dollars to new development; need for flexibility in CIP administration
	Tax increment financing	Larger projects, especially mixed use	Legal limitations in most states
	Special improvement districts	Commercial and industrial areas covering both infill and rehabilitation	Taxpayers must be willing to participate
	Greater flexibility and creativity in plan review	All infill projects	Resistance from city public works/ engineering staff to deviation from "standards"

Identifying Infill Opportunities

Effective infill policies and programs must be based on a sound understanding of the quantity of infill land, its key characteristics (location, size, ownership, availability, market attractiveness, zoning, and physical limitations), and the development economics. As established earlier, infill land exists in a variety of forms—in scattered locations or concentrated in a few neighborhoods, in large tracts, and in individual home lots. Also, the economics of infilling can vary among communities and among individual parcels, as is demonstrated in Part II of this book. Before communities act to limit further urbanization of rural lands, they should be certain that the infill land supply—physically developable, in marketable locations, and available for sale or lease by owners—is sufficient to prevent undue price increases. On the other hand, planners should not underestimate infill opportunities lest public resources be spent on providing additional urban-type services at the metropolitan fringe when they are not really needed.

Vacant land inventories have been conducted over the past few years by regional planning agencies, cities and counties, and such private organizations as Chambers of Commerce or housing advocacy groups. These research efforts cover entire regions, individual communities, or specific neighborhoods where special attention to vacant, skipped-over land seems appropriate. In some cases, they are based on complete canvasses of all vacant land. In others, a sample is used, or the focus is narrowed to land suitable for industry or assisted housing. All parcels may be included, or attention may be focused on only large tracts of five or more acres. Data sources range from field surveys to aerial photography to tax assessors' files.

Originally, efforts to determine quantities of vacant land were incidental to comprehensive land use inventories used for community and regional planning. Increasingly, special attention has been focused on vacant land in heavily urbanized areas, resulting in sophisticated vacant land inventories with extensive data available on an individual parcel basis or by census tract, square mile, or other planning area designation.

These inventories can be expensive to compile and to update in an era of limited budgets for research and planning, especially at the regional level. It is important, therefore, that the scope of an inventory be appropriate to local needs and objectives. The methods used will vary depending on whether vacant land data will be used to:

- formulate or assess regional development strategies and alternative plans
- promote municipal economic development
- identify areas suitable for new housing
- revise zoning map designations
- provide information to builders and developers.

This chapter provides examples of inventory techniques tailored to varying regional and municipal needs, covering methods of measuring the infill land supply on a regional, county, or municipal scale. Alternative approaches and data sources are discussed, and examples of inventories undertaken by various agencies are described. In addition, the preparation and use of infill parcel files as a way of providing information on development opportunities is discussed.

For those localities that are unable to undertake areawide surveys or prepare parcel files, this chapter suggests ways to identify rapidly some target neighborhoods and sites for which public action to promote infilling may be appropriate. An effort has been made to document costs incurred by planning and community development agencies who have studied vacant land and to include low-cost approaches. Planners always should be aware of the trade-offs between cost and time and comprehensiveness.

No discussion of inventory methods would be complete without examining how the results of vacant land surveys are disseminated. They can be used by elected officials to set development policy or by staff to familiarize private developers with infill opportunities. The descriptions of local efforts include parcel files and data banks open to the public, as well as land supply/demand studies used to set holding zones, urban boundaries, or service limit lines.

Calculating the Amount of Vacant Land

In discussing various methods and techniques for determining the amount of vacant land, attention should be focused on the type of information that can be collected, the degree of detail available on individual parcels or tracts of land, and system costs. Creating any type of land use information system is costly. Proposals for establishing new systems may be rejected because of staffing requirements for data collection or coding, and existing systems may become useless because updating is infeasible. Figure 2-1 summarizes methods used by 11 agencies across the country to measure vacant land and to determine its characteristics. Detailed information on these examples is provided later in this chapter.

Using Existing Land Use Information

For regional assessments of vacant land quantities, the simplest (and perhaps least costly) technique would be to use existing land use data and maps that have already been prepared for other planning purposes. This approach makes sense where agencies lack the resources for new aerial photos or where land use information is fairly current. Quantities of vacant land, if not already tabulated by the individual communities, can be determined by relatively inexperienced planning staff using planimeters or other scaling measures. Because land use mapping efforts are designed to meet many planning needs—not just identification of infill land—the researcher may not be able to learn very much about the nature of vacant property (its physical characteristics, environmental constraints, or ownership characteristics). Because of these limitations, planning agencies have looked for ways to improve the quality of information obtained about vacant acreage, regardless of whether it is collected as part of an overall land use planning effort or in a separate vacant land inventory.

Aerial Photography

One means of improving information is through the use of aerial photography. Vacant tracts can be pin-pointed on aerial photos and then transferred to base maps for further analysis. Aerials are also useful in public presentations. Overlay maps depicting conditions, such as floodplains, steep slopes, major infrastructure, etc. can be readily prepared at the same scale.

One major drawback in using aerials for identifying infill land is that high costs and limited staff time often preclude identification of small vacant parcels. Vacant land surveys based on aerial photography generally do not include parcels under two acres in size, and most identify only tracts of five acres or more. Significant infill opportunities can be overlooked as a result. It should be noted, however, that aerial photography technology is constantly improving, allowing greater identification of detail than was possible 10 years ago.

Aerial photography is one means of improving information on vacant parcels.

Aside from the costs and staff time, measuring vacant land quantities from aerial photos—even at a scale of five acres or more—is a time-consuming and often tedious task, especially for a large urban county or region. In the past, planning agencies employed students, interns, or trainees to do this work. In the future, it may be difficult for agencies to find the resources needed for such labor-intensive activities.

As a result, a conscious decision to overlook sites of under two acres may be prudent in multicounty land use inventories. Identifying and measuring small, single lot tracts, incapable of accommodating much of the region's development needs, may not be cost effective. This is especially true for special-purpose vacant land inventories designed to identify sites suitable for industrial development. On the other hand, individual cities or suburbs may well want to make a special effort to locate small lots, especially if they are heavily built up and lack large vacant tracts. These properties can be developed with new housing that is compatible with surrounding older buildings.

Measuring vacant land shown on aerial photographs will not, in and of itself, provide much of the information useful to planners in determining development potential. Ideally, the vacant tracts should be noted on parcel or plat maps, which will allow planning staff to determine more easily the jurisdictional boundaries and census tracts (for tabulation purposes). Once the sites are mapped, it is possible to determine whether vacant areas consist of one or multiple parcels and to check whether the parcels are in single or multiple ownership. For those planning agencies that do not have direct access to computerized deed recording or tax assessment files, this task will usually involve first looking up the legal descriptions or tax identification numbers and then checking ownership records.

Figure 2-1
Summary of Key Characteristics of Vacant Land Inventories

	County and Regional Inventories				Municipal Inventories						
	Twin Cities Metro Council	Miami Valley RPC	Lane Council of Governments	Metropolitan Service District	King County, WA	Denver, CO	Wilmington, DE	Washington, DC	Toledo, OH	Dallas, TX	Milwaukee, WI
Coverage:											
All land uses	X	X	X	X		X		X			X
Vacant land only					X		X		X	X	
Sources:											
Land use maps	X			X	X						
Aerial photos	X	X	X		X				X		
Assessors' files			X			X	X	X			X
Field surveys		X		X			X		X		
Tabulation By:											
Parcel			X			X	X	X		X	X
Census block			X			X				X	X
Census tract		X	X	X	X	X			X	X	X
Neighborhood or planning area						X			X	X	
Jurisdiction/ political boundaries		X	X	X	X	X					X
Section/township/range					X						
Traffic zone		X									
Watershed		X									
Information Collected:											
Zoning		X	X			X	X	X	X	X	X
Planned use		X	X								
Utility service		X	X							X	
Road access			X							X	
Physical limitations	X	X	X	X					X		
Parcel size			X			X	X	X		X	X
Owner name/ address						X	X			X	X
Assessed value						X					X
Tax delinquency							X	X			
Tax-exempt sites											X
Public ownership				X				X			
Recent sale information						X		X			X

Source: Real Estate Research Corporation

Tax Assessors' Files

Alternatively, the first step in conducting the vacant land inventory could be to use tax assessment records as the primary data source, as was done in the three case studies. Vacant parcels can be identified from tax records in one of two ways: through land use codes that indicate the development status of each parcel or by looking at the assessed value of improvements. Where improvement value is zero, the property can be assumed to be vacant.

Although assessors' records eliminate some of the problems associated with aerial photos, they have their own unique limitations as well. The major benefits of assessors' records are:

- availability of computerized records in many urban counties. Information on vacant land found on cards, tape, or disc can be copied for use by planning researchers. These systems can usually be programmed to yield data for an entire county, a town, or even smaller geographic units. The cost of obtaining such information is usually minimal. However, the cost of writing the necessary computer programs must be considered.
- tie-in to additional information on parcel ownership, size, and assessed valuation. Information on zoning, plan designations, and physical or service attributes may also be available in the same files.

However, systems used by assessors are anything but uniform. They are designed to meet the tax-levying functions of local government and not planning functions. Some of the problems encountered include:

- unwillingness or inability of assessors' staff to provide data in a form usable by planners. Information on the assessed values of vacant land can be politically sensitive, causing reluctance on the part of assessors to distribute data that could be analyzed on anything but a lot-by-lot basis.
- lack of comparability among systems. In a region with more than one assessing jurisdiction, computer or manual record-keeping systems may not be compatible, making it difficult to produce a consistent regionwide analysis.
- lack of complete information. Information on vacant parcels can be particularly spotty. Key data such as parcel dimensions may be missing. Location-related variables will be limited. For example, unsubdivided vacant tracts may not have street addresses or other codes, such as zip code or census tract, making it difficult to find the parcels on maps.

- need to cross-reference with other data files. Not all of the useful information will always be contained on a single file.
- time lag in file updating. Assessors' records usually lag well behind current construction and demolition activity. Files may not be updated until six months or so after a building is completed or demolished. In an active real estate market, infill parcels listed as vacant by the assessor may have construction under way or recently finished. A truly accurate picture of the quantity of infill land will require checking against recent aerial photos or field verification. Because field work can be very time-consuming and expensive, agencies may want to consider drawing a sample of parcels for field checking and then adjust overall estimates of vacant land quantities accordingly.
- tax parcels not always buildable lots. Some parcels listed as vacant on the tax rolls could be: public parks or open space (may be coded as tax exempt); right-of-way remnants (may be coded as tax exempt); utility easements; or yards, driveways, or parking spaces belonging to buildings that occupy more than one tax lot. These conditions may not be evident until tax roll information is mapped or field-verified. However, eliminating all tax-exempt properties is *not* a good solution. It would result in dropping surplus lands owned by government agencies or not-for-profit institutions that might be available for development.

Field Surveys

In small cities and suburbs, or for individual neighborhoods in larger cities, a 100 percent field canvass of vacant land may be a reasonable level of effort. Using existing parcel maps, two-person teams can conduct windshield surveys to identify vacant tracts. If assessors' file data are also available, they could be plotted first on the map so as to focus the windshield survey on those streets and blocks that are most likely to contain vacant land.

In addition to marking vacant parcels on the maps, the field surveying team can observe the physical character of the land. The nature of adjacent uses can be noted as can amenities, such as nearby parks or attractive views. For more extensive analyses, the field staff may want to make note of the condition of streets that abut infill parcels and the level of maintenance of surrounding buildings. Relatively inexperienced students or interns will need training in how to make these admittedly subjective assessments. Use of slides or photographs that illustrate how to rate physical conditions can be helpful and will result in more consistent responses among a number of field staff. Figure 2-2 suggests information that can be obtained by trained observers as part of field surveying.

Using Samples

As indicated above, budget limitations and other considerations may dictate examining a sample of infill parcels, rather than doing a 100 percent canvass. If a sample is properly drawn, it can be used to make reasonable inferences about infill land quantities and key characteristics.

Samples can be taken from either aerial photos or tax records, but the methods are dramatically different. Planners should consult with agency staff members or outside experts from local universities or research firms to assure that the sample is properly drawn and sufficient in size to meet local objectives.

Obviously, there are trade-offs between the degree of precision desired and the resources available to most planning or community development agencies. The size of the sample and the methods used to draw it will also depend on the number of parcel "subgroups" for which information is desired—i.e., infill land zoned for housing versus land zoned for industrial use; parcels in the central city versus suburban locations; large tracts and single lots.

Given that assessors' files are not up to date, any sample drawn from tax records should be significantly larger than will be needed ultimately to allow for sites that are no longer vacant. Depending on how the research program is structured, other sampled sites may also be eliminated from the final group of sites that are studied in detail. As mentioned earlier, publicly owned land in permanent open space, utility easements, rights-of-way, or other undevelopable vacant tracts probably do not warrant detailed research. Some jurisdictions will not want to consider environmentally constrained land.

If assessors' files are used as the source of the sample, it may not be possible to identify these limiting conditions until the parcels are mapped or field inspected. Of a

---

Figure 2-2
Characteristics of Infill Parcels That Can Be Observed in Field Inspections

Physical Characteristics
- Parcel shape (rectangular, square, pie, or wedge, irregular)
- Street access (whether site has direct frontage on public streets)
- Presence of any structures that could limit development (such as electric transmission towers or oil/gas pumps)
- Site vegetation
- Obvious terrain or topographic limitations
- Presence of foundations left from previous buildings

Location Amenities
- Proximity to parks, transit, highways, shopping, etc.
- Possibility of attractive views
- Waterfront location

Neighborhood Conditions
- Condition of streets, sidewalks, and other public areas
- Exterior maintenance level of nearby buildings
- Presence of nearby abandoned or underutilized buildings
- Nature of surrounding land uses

Land Availability
- Whether or not a site is posted with a "for sale or lease" sign
- Name and phone number of owner or agent listed on signs (sources of additional information if needed)

sample of 53 lots in Knoxville listed as vacant on the tax rolls, Knoxville-Knox County Planning Commission planning staff found that:

- Twenty-one were not vacant anymore.
- Twelve were subject to severe physical constraints (steep slope, shale deposits, sinkholes, or flooding).
- Four were deemed too small to be developable.
- Three had inadequate utilities.
- Thirteen were developable infill sites.

Determining Service Availability

Service availability and capacity can vary widely within urbanized areas. Not all vacant parcels in central cities or older suburbs will have access to full services. For example, sites with unusual terrain or topography may not have direct access to water and sewer lines, even though other nearby built-up properties are served. Other parcels may have originally been planned for low-density single-family development using septic tanks rather than public sewers, but today's land prices may dictate higher density development that would need sewer extensions. Some sites may have utilities but lack proximity to fire stations. Others may be landlocked, lacking direct frontage on public streets.

In assessing the quantity of infill land and the potential benefits of its use for a city, these service limitations must be realistically evaluated. Again, planning agencies may lack the funds to do a complete parcel-by-parcel analysis of service availability and adequacy. In addition, infrastructure adequacy must often be evaluated on a neighborhood, community, or regional scale rather than at the individual site level. For example, a vacant site may have city water lines at the property line, but the size of the water main and the adequacy of pressure levels in the surrounding neighborhood may well determine whether a given proposed development can hook up without making off-site improvements. Whether a given elementary school system will have the capacity to support additional pupils generated by infill housing will depend on pupil assignment policies, state or locally mandated limits on class size, and the condition of older school buildings. One small infill housing development is unlikely to overload a school system, but housing construction on every infill site in a given attendance area or district could pose problems.

Once infill land has been located on base maps, it is possible to prepare overlays (at the same scale) depicting service availability. The key items noted in a regional or community inventory should be:

- sewer interceptors
- water mains
- schools and their service areas
- fire stations
- expressways and major arterials.

In addition, some jurisdictions will want to note transit lines and stops, police substations, public libraries, and parks. Local standards for service access can then be applied. These standards will vary among regions and among individual jurisdictions within regions; they may have to be generalized to make a multi-jurisdiction assessment reasonable.

Planning documents (such as 201 wastewater facilities plans or highway maps) and conversations with department staff are the best sources of information on service availability and adequacy. In a regional study, a large number of small special-purpose districts may have to be contacted. Using earlier plans can avoid duplication of effort. For example, 201 plans prepared for the U.S. Environmental Protection Agency (EPA) usually indicate in general terms areas that are served by public sewers, as well as pinpointing areas with localized problems, such as collapsed sewers. This level of detail may be sufficient, especially when obtaining information on parcel-specific utility service throughout a county or region requires examining the maps of numerous separate sewer districts.

Recent national studies have raised the issue of infrastructure condition, as well as capacity in assessing the development potential of infill sites. News articles have documented the lack of investment in public facilities maintenance, especially in older cities with declining resources, where the problems are most acute. There is no way to generalize the extent to which infill development potential is limited because of maintenance neglect. In some cities, historical records on the age of utility lines and roads are spotty. Age is not always a good measure for infrastructure condition, which will vary based on weather, usage, and ongoing maintenance practices.

Undersized or inadequately maintained systems may not constrain development, particularly development of small-scale projects. In strong markets, developers of larger projects may be willing to undertake infrastructure upgrading; in weaker markets, local government may have to invest in repairs or replacement before private investment will occur.

Analyzing the adequacy of utilities, roads, and other public facilities and services is a major undertaking that should be a part of ongoing capital improvement programming and service delivery analyses. Planners will usually have to rely on earlier studies or the opinions of senior engineers or facilities programming staff.

Assessing Physical Limitations

Many regional land use inventories contain detailed information on key physical attributes of vacant land. The purpose of such analyses is to identify whether physical limitations of vacant sites are so significant as to constrain or even prohibit development. The most commonly noted sites with environmental problems are those located "in the floodplain." Planning agencies often map both vacant land and developed areas that lie within the 100-year floodplain, although this standard is by no means universal. The second most commonly noted limitation is "steep slope," but what is considered steep in a relatively flat part of the country may be quite different than in areas where development commonly occurs on hilly or rugged terrain. Other physical/ environmental factors that can be included in vacant land studies are listed in Figure 2-3.

Planners and engineers will want to ensure that infill development on very steep slopes does not cause landslide hazards or that development of land in the floodplain does not increase downstream flooding. In less extreme situations, local officials will merely want to assure that development on these unusual sites is sensitive to the problems that might occur.

The lack of clear standards for determining what land is "developable" from a physical/environmental perspective poses significant problems in interpreting the results of vacant land inventories. For example, if planners choose not to count vacant infill land in the 100-year floodplain, they will underestimate infill development potential as long as local ordinances permit at least some urban uses on flood-prone land. On the other hand, environmentally sensitive sites cannot be expected to develop at the same intensity as nearby sites lacking development constraints.

Information on physical and environmental limitations to development is available from a variety of sources, as indicated in Figure 2-4. Data collected for other planning and engineering purposes will usually be sufficient to identify the presence of environmental limitations on a broad scale, but may not be sufficient for evaluating individual parcels.

There are other environmental issues that may be peculiar to a given region and not widespread across the county. For example, some regions suffer from land subsidence (sinking due to withdrawal and nonreplenishment of groundwater supplies). Another possible concern could be buried hazardous wastes or archeological sites, the locations of which have yet to be thoroughly documented in many communities.

Figure 2-3
Physical/Environmental Information Commonly Found in Vacant Land Studies

- Location of flood-prone sites and wetlands
- Steeply sloped land
- Land subject to slide hazard
- Earthquake-prone sites
- Sites with shallow depth to bedrock or other soils "buildability" limitations
- Land prone to subsidence
- Land unsuitable for housing because of its location in airport-landing flight paths
- Land in air pollution nonattainment areas
- Prime agricultural land
- Unusual natural habitats

Figure 2-4
Sources of Information on Physical/Environmental Constraints to Development

Condition	Data Source
Flood-prone areas	HUD Flood Insurance Program Maps
Steep slopes	U.S. Geological Survey Topographic Maps; LANDSAT data (satellite photography)
Soils buildability	U.S. Department of Agriculture Soil Conservation Service Maps (usually do not cover central cities); state agriculture or natural resource departments
Landslide hazard areas	U.S. Geological Survey Maps on slope, combined with Soil Conservation Service notation of unstable soils
Noise and vibration	Airport master plans; Federal Aviation Administration
Air pollution	Air quality plans noting point sources and nonattainment areas
Septic tank suitability	201 wastewater facilities plans; local health agency data

Determining Current Zoning

In order to compare the infill land supply with probable development-related demand, it is important to examine current zoning. Many jurisdictions have curtailed the development potential of their infill land by failing to match zoning to demand for various types of development and densities. The relative ease or difficulty encountered by builders requesting zoning changes varies among communities, but obtaining a use change or variance can be a time-consuming, costly procedure that could discourage infilling.

Some inventories try to measure precisely the amount of vacant land in each zone. Others will assign to a tract whatever designation covers the largest amount of its land area. Again, there is a trade-off between precision, available staff resources, and time committed to the vacant land inventory.

Studies that cover multiple jurisdictions will need to standardize their zoning categories. One way to do this is to translate each zone designation into a density range. For example, a parcel zoned R-2 in Suburb X would be counted as "single-family, 4–6 d.u. (dwelling units)/acre," as could a parcel zoned RS 8000 in Suburb Y. The number of classifications will depend on the degree of detail required. A simple system would designate parcels as single-family, multifamily, commercial, industrial, and "other" (to cover special designations or PUDs). Where agricultural or open space zoning is found within the urbanized area, these categories should also be noted.

In some jurisdictions, it may be more useful to categorize a parcel by its land use designation in adopted plans rather than its current zoning. This would be useful in communities where:

- Plan designations take precedence over zoning by law (as is the case in Oregon and California).
- Plans have recently been adopted, but zoning revisions have not yet been made to implement the plans.
- Zoning changes are readily obtainable.

Ascertaining the Availability of Infill Land

To quantify the infill land supply realistically, it is important to survey infill landowners to find out why they hold land and what they plan to do with their land (if anything). Very few planning agencies have taken their research this far. As a result, the available vacant land supply tends to be overestimated.

The motives and plans of infill landowners can be assessed through brief surveys, which can be administered by mail or by telephone. It is not necessary to survey all property owners; a representative sample should be sufficient. A mail survey will require a larger sample because high response rates cannot be assured, but it will be less costly to administer than a telephone survey that requires repeated callbacks. The researcher will want to be certain that mail-in responses are not skewed geographically or in other ways critical to drawing reasonable inferences. For example, responses should be checked to assure that owners of large parcels are not dramatically overrepresented among respondents. Call-backs or second mailings may be needed.

In jurisdictions with computerized property records, it may be possible to obtain a computer-generated sample of vacant lots that includes the name and address of the owner or agent who receives property tax bills). Some systems can even generate mailing labels. In most cases, however, ownership will have to be looked up manually.

In allocating staff time and budgets, planners should recognize that some phone numbers will be difficult or impossible to track down (i.e., out-of-town owners, corporate subsidiaries not separately listed in phone directories, individuals with unlisted numbers). Some owners or their representatives will be unwilling to cooperate with survey researchers. This is especially true in states such as Illinois and Florida, where owners can establish blind land trusts at local banks in order to protect their identities. Bank officers will be extremely reluctant to divulge any information about trust-protected parcels of their owners.

Talking to owners can yield valuable information that will help set appropriate development policy. Figure 2-5 suggests basic questions that could be asked of infill landowners. If it is feasible to administer a longer survey, other questions could be added. Owners of available properties might be asked to:

- assess strengths and weaknesses of their sites from a market perspective
- verify information obtained from secondary sources regarding physical limitations or ownership of adjacent lots
- discuss how they are marketing their land
- suggest the types of uses most likely to be built
- comment on adequacy of zoning, public facilities, or other government roles in the development process.

Figure 2-5
Interview Questions for Infill Landowners

1. Is the owner
   —An individual or group of individuals?
   —A business partnership or corporation?
   —An institution, such as a hospital or religious order?
   —A government agency?
2. How long has the present owner held the property?
3. Why has the land remained vacant?
   —The owner plans to develop it eventually.
   —The land is being held for long-term appreciation.
   —The market is weak (prices are depressed).
   —The land is being kept vacant for personal reasons (desire for privacy, family use, etc.).
   —Title is not clear.
   —The land is held for future government use.
   —The land is being held for expansion of adjacent businesses.
   —The land is used for parking.
4. Are any plans to develop the land presently pending?
5. If not, does the owner envision developing the land within five years or selling/leasing the land for development by others?
6. If the land is presently available for sale or lease, what is the asking price/rent?

Owners who are currently unwilling to develop, sell, or lease their land could be asked what, if anything, would encourage them to sell or to lease their property. All landowners are not equally knowledgeable about the requirements of successful real estate development. Asking owners of isolated vacant lots that are *not* available for development to assess the market for their land would yield dubious results.

Tabulating responses on land availability gives a one-time snapshot of owner plans. Plans can change quickly with shifts in the general economy, the real estate market, or personal/business circumstances. In addition, parcels deemed available could be unrealistically priced and hence unattractive to developers. Determining the reasonableness of asking prices or rents for hundreds of parcels will be impossible for most planning or economic development agencies.

The following pages offer examples of a few of the more advanced vacant land inventory techniques. For each system, information is provided on data sources, geographic coverage, data items included, frequency of updating, and costs. (It should be stressed that none of these systems considers marketability or availability of the sites it identifies.) The rationale for establishing the inventory and its use by both public officials and the private sector are described. References are listed for those readers who require additional information.

Objectives. To provide information useful in the formulation of new land use policies and regulations, to monitor the effect of county policies and land use regulations on the land market, and to indicate when changes in county land use regulations may be needed.

Data Sources. Plat maps noting vacant land, as derived from aerial photographs. Each map covers ½-section (½-square-mile).

Coverage. The developable portion of King County (800 square miles) west of the Cascade Mountains.

Information Collected for Vacant Land.
Acreage
Zoning
Acreage with no physical hazards (including steep slopes, wetlands, and severe potential for earthquake damage)
Section/township/range
Jurisdiction
Census tract
Plat map page

Updating. Annually, using building permits. Information is 6–10 months out of date. Original inventory used 1977 data but did not cover the city of Seattle and certain incorporated suburbs.

Costs.
Original Data Collection:
Two full-time planners for one year
Three technical assistants for six months each
Individual cities and towns also contributed additional staff time.

Updates:
Two technical assistants full-time for six months each
Part-time supervision from a senior staff person

Computer Costs:
$2,000 per year
Ongoing Operations and Data Retrieval (Covers both Building Permit and Vacant Land Systems): One full-time planner, three technical assistants, and $10,000 in computer expenses per year.

Dissemination. Published vacant land inventory is available for purchase. Acreage is tabulated by municipality, section/township/range, major zoning groupings, and presence/absence of severe development constraints.

Use by Elected Officials. In preparing the comprehensive plan and community plans.

Use by Private Interests. Come in to look at maps to identify vacant land.

Contact.
Sharron Shinbo
King County Division of Planning
W217 King County Courthouse
516 3rd Avenue
Seattle, Washington 98104
(206) 344-7550

Objectives. Basis for update of city's master plan. Also to identify vacant land parcels and encourage development within the city.

Data Sources. Aerial photographs and field check. Data transferred onto land use maps.

Coverage. Entire city of Toledo. Includes parcels of at least two acres. Toledo covers about 84.8 square miles.

Information Collected.
Location (neighborhood, street address)
Census tract
Acreage
Floodplain status
Zoning
Development problems (i.e., physical and locational impediments such as large ditches and creeks, unusual configuration, and lack of roadway frontage)
Keyed to pages in atlas map system

Update. Original study in 1974. Update in 1977.

Costs. 1974 Inventory: Two students collected the data during the summer months. 1977 Inventory: One planner worked one month checking for changes in status from the previous inventory.

Dissemination to the Public. Compiled into a publication that is available upon request. Tabulations are available by neighborhood.

Use by Elected Officials. Updating of master plan (which has not been accepted yet).

Use by Private Interests. Special requests from developers are honored.

Problems Encountered. Property lines and ownership patterns cannot be distinguished.

Contact.
Walter Edelen, Executive Director
Toledo City Planning Commission
415 N. St. Clair Street
Toledo, Ohio 43604
(419) 247-6280

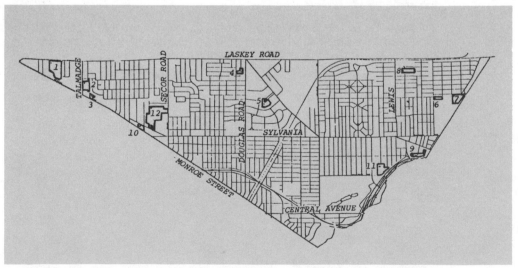

West Toledo, Ohio, vacant land inventory, with infill locations numbered.

Objectives. System was first formulated in the 1970s to identify target areas of the city for the community renewal program. Also general information support for planning activities.

Data Sources. Real Estate Master File of assessor. Also used an Address Coding Guide.

Coverage. All of the city and county of Denver. Both vacant and developed parcels.

Information Collected for Vacant Land.
Vacant land use
Street address
Assessor's number
Zoning
Parcel size
Assessed value
Last three sales dates
Tax-exempt status
Last three sales amounts
X/Y coordinates
Census tract and block
Neighborhood Council District

Updating. Annual. Update is accomplished by creating a new extract from the assessor's file and then going through an internal maintenance routine to modify the records.

Costs. No estimate of the initial start-up costs is available. Updating costs: $5,000 for data processing and about $5,400 in labor costs. (Two full-time staff who devote 10 percent of their time to the update.)

Dissemination. Summaries are disseminated through publications of the department. Standard reports, with more complete records, are available for perusal by the public in the planning office.

Use by Elected Officials.
Comprehensive plan update
Neighborhood plans
Housing allocation planning
Rezoning requests
Population modeling
Special requests

Use by Private Interests. Special requests including site selection, real estate, and development studies.

Problems Encountered. Difficult to do time series analysis because of changes in the assessor's coding systems.

Contact.
Dave Turk
Information Services Section
Denver Planning Office
Denver, Colorado 80202
(303) 575-3375

Objectives. Monitoring development; producing a general land use information base; providing a historic time series to use in development forecast models.

Data Sources. Aerial photographs (most recently at 1″ = 800″). Augmented by tabulations from previous inventories, historical aerials, building permit data, field checking, and maps.

Coverage. Entire 3,000-square-mile metropolitan area. Both vacant and developed properties.

Information Collected for Vacant Land. Suitability for development (presence/absence of swamps or steep slopes)
Suitability for expansion of adjacent development.

Updating. Every two to four years, depending on budget resources. First inventory conducted in 1958. Last update in 1981, covering 1978 to 1980 period.

Costs. The 1978 aerial photographs cost $24,000 (200 prints for 3,000 square miles). Costs were shared with other users.

1979 Labor:
One Planning assistant for one year
One Supervisor for two months
Planner/assistants for 3–4 months of tabulations and report writing
Planning assistant/draftsman for six months of mapping
$5,000 for 4,000 copies of the printed report
$2,500 for work materials
Funding sources were not specified.

Dissemination. A generalized land use map of the region, produced once every eight or 10 years. Municipal maps of each update. Report of basic land use trends, tabulated by major geocodes, including county, city, ring, and sector. The four rings are central city, fully developed suburbs, developing suburbs, and the outer area. Eight suburban sectors radiate from the central cities. Prints of aerial photographs available at cost. Specific analysis reports which focus on the monitoring and policy aspects of the land use data.

Use by Elected Officials. Used to summarize land use in the region. Monitor development for conformance with council policy plans. Monitor development process to improve forecasting capabilities.

Contact.
Michael Munson
Program Manager for Research
Metropolitan Council of the Twin Cities
300 Metro Square Building
7th and Robert
St. Paul, Minnesota 55101
(612) 291–6331

Objectives. To develop a monitoring system for land use changes and to keep track of vacant land and vacant land prices. Also to evaluate the effect of the region's urban growth boundary on land prices.

Data Sources. Primarily aerial photographs at a scale of 1″ = 2,000′. Also used local inventories, field surveys, and building permit records. Information transferred to street base maps. The data are considered accurate for planning at the census tract level.

Coverage. Entire metropolitan area of 250,000 acres. Vacant and developed uses.

Information Collected for Vacant Land.
Acreage tabulation
Sewer availability
Water availability
Public ownership
Hazard areas
Planned use
Jurisdiction
Census tracts
Urban growth boundary
Vacant land quantities are tabulated by zoning and by whether land is located in a physical hazard area.

Updating. First prepared in 1977. One update prepared in 1979–80 using 1978 aerial photographs. Future updates depend on budget availability.

Costs.
1977 Inventory: Project director: .5 person year; lead technical staff: .9 person year; data collectors and measures: 2.6 person years. Total Cost: $45,000, of which $26,000 was for direct labor, $2,000 for fringe benefits, $12,000 for overhead. Maps, photographs, other materials, and computer services cost $5,000.

Update Cost (1979 actual, 1980 projected): Two person years; $40,250 including fringe benefits and indirect costs

Dissemination. Maps are available at a scale of 1″ = 2,000′, as are tabulations by census tract and jurisdiction.

Use by Elected Officials. Used as a tool to monitor development trends and adjust urban growth boundary. Also used in making public investment decisions (i.e., transportation planning; special market analyses for light rail and regional shopping centers).

Contact.
Neal Van Horn
Metropolitan Service District
527 Southwest Hall
Portland, Oregon 97201
(503) 221-1646

Objectives. Environmental information for the 208 Water Quality Management program.

Data Sources. Aerial photographs were a primary data source (LANDSAT photos used for rural areas). Field surveys, records, and maps for specialized data such as flooding, soils, slope, etc. (USGS, SCS maps, state's Department of Natural Resources, university geologists' studies).

Coverage. The entire five-county Miami Valley surrounding Dayton. Mapped at scale of 1″ = 4,000′.

Information Collected for Vacant Land.
Land use (vacant land is counted together with agricultural land).
Soil information
Landcover (forest, grasslands, water, agriculture)
Slope
Groundwater availability
Bedrock depth
Natural areas
Historic and archeological sites
Geocoding (political boundaries, watersheds, traffic zones, census tracts)
The system uses a linear regression model to indicate suitability for development using over 30 variables. A series of computer-generated maps was prepared for each county.

Updating. Data were collected in 1975 but have not been updated.

Costs. Costs were shared by the state and the Miami Valley Regional Planning Commission. The state covered the aerial photography and remote sensing costs and developed the system. RPC staff interpreted the aerials. Although staff could not indicate total expenditures for this effort, they feel it was very costly and as a result may not be updated.

Dissemination. Agency files are available to the public for data inspection. Special reports have been released by both the regional planning agency and the Ohio Department of Natural Resources, which uses this system elsewhere in the state.

Use by Elected Officials.
Data for the 208 Water Quality Management program; the Development Guidelines Atlas, showing existing land use and potential land use (including housing); and in revising Miami Valley land use plan.

Use by Private Interests. Special requests are honored. The MVRPC's Development Guidelines map packet is available for each of the five counties.

Contact.
Karen Adams
Miami Valley Regional Planning Commission
117 South Main
Dayton, Ohio 45402
(513) 223-6323

Development of a Model for Residential Land Use

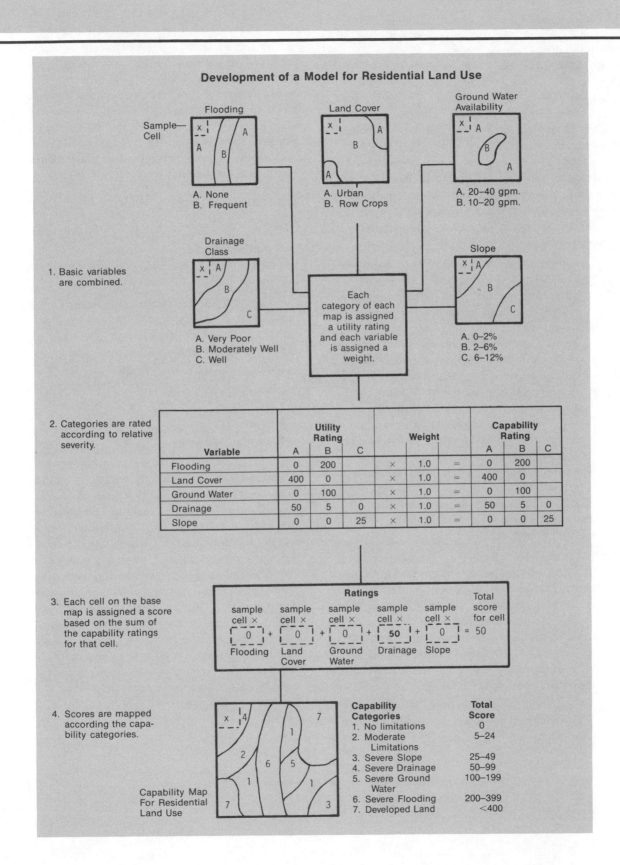

1. Basic variables are combined.

Flooding
- A. None
- B. Frequent

Land Cover
- A. Urban
- B. Row Crops

Ground Water Availability
- A. 20–40 gpm.
- B. 10–20 gpm.

Drainage Class
- A. Very Poor
- B. Moderately Well
- C. Well

Slope
- A. 0–2%
- B. 2–6%
- C. 6–12%

Each category of each map is assigned a utility rating and each variable is assigned a weight.

2. Categories are rated according to relative severity.

Variable	Utility Rating			Weight			Capability Rating		
	A	B	C				A	B	C
Flooding	0	200		×	1.0	=	0	200	
Land Cover	400	0		×	1.0	=	400	0	
Ground Water	0	100		×	1.0	=	0	100	
Drainage	50	5	0	×	1.0	=	50	5	0
Slope	0	0	25	×	1.0	=	0	0	25

3. Each cell on the base map is assigned a score based on the sum of the capability ratings for that cell.

Ratings

					Total score for cell
sample cell ×	sample cell ×	sample cell ×	sample cell ×	sample cell ×	
0	+ 0	+ 0	+ 50	+ 0	= 50
Flooding	Land Cover	Ground Water	Drainage	Slope	

4. Scores are mapped according the capability categories.

Capability Map For Residential Land Use

Capability Categories	Total Score
1. No limitations	0
2. Moderate Limitations	5–24
3. Severe Slope	25–49
4. Severe Drainage	50–99
5. Severe Ground Water	100–199
6. Severe Flooding	200–399
7. Developed Land	<400

Creating an Infill Parcel File

As indicated earlier, most regional and municipal vacant land inventories focus on aggregate quantities of vacant land and their physical suitability for development. While useful for preparing comprehensive plans and development strategies, data tabulated only at the municipal (or even census tract) level are of little use to developers considering alternative building sites. Infill policies can be implemented only if developers become aware of and are willing to work with individual infill properties. For this reason, a few cities have instituted systems that can provide detailed information on individual vacant parcels. This type of site-specific data is especially useful to small builders lacking sufficient support staff to search out vacant sites and identify their key characteristics.

Parcel files are usually, but not exclusively, maintained by city governments or special purpose development authorities rather than regional planning agencies. Larger cities have recently instituted automated retrieval systems that provide computer printouts of key facts about all of the vacant lots in a given neighborhood, census tract, or block. Data on a particular parcel can also be retrieved if identifier codes are known (these can usually be looked up on plat maps). Parcel files are generally adapted from tax assessment or deed records and are updated periodically using subdivision, building, or demolition permits. Some jurisdictions update their systems quarterly, while most make changes annually. The most sophisticated systems, such as the one used in Eugene, Oregon, allow planning staff to sit at a video display terminal and receive instant information on vacant lots. The simplest systems have basic information recorded manually on index cards or lists.

Municipal parcel files are not always comprehensive. Cities with scarce resources or limited data processing capabilities may choose to focus on special needs or development opportunities. Inventories of sites available for industrial use are most common. This information is made available to promote economic development and job generation. Local Chambers of Commerce and electric utility companies often sponsor or assist with maintaining industrial parcel files.

Another type of special purpose file lists vacant parcels suitable for low- and moderate-income housing. County and regional planning agencies or fair housing groups sponsor creation of these files to encourage deconcentration of subsidized units and to identify locations that might be "ready to go" as subsidy funds become available.

City real estate departments typically collect a wide variety of information concerning municipally owned land that might be made available to private developers or to community groups willing and able to improve and maintain property. Rarely, however, do these files include sites owned by other nonmunicipal public agencies (such as school districts, the state, or the federal government). As a result, they may not provide complete listings of all government-owned land.

Information Typically Provided In Parcel Files

A number of examples of vacant parcel file data are provided in the following pages to illustrate the types of information collected. Most systems include:

- a parcel identifier number (tax or map number)
- the street address
- the lot size or dimensions
- the owner's name.

More sophisticated files will add:

- zoning designations
- planned use
- the owner's address
- assessed valuation
- utility service availability.

The specifics vary from city to city. Wilmington, Delaware, for example, inputs the results of field inspection, rating maintenance conditions for both the vacant lot and the block on which it is located. Wilmington's system notes whether the lots were filled with trash or being used for parking and how many years of back taxes were outstanding. Dallas provides the parcel's legal description, census tract and block identifiers, street frontage lengths, and street improvements. Files specifically tailored to industrial development needs will usually note whether or not a particular site has rail access. Distance to expressways and the size/capacity characteristics of electrical service or water mains may be noted. Housing files might note the character of adjacent development and the distance to shopping, schools, or transit.

In some cases, parcel files will also cite development constraints, such as location in the floodplain or odd, irregular shape. The purpose of the file and the ways in which it will be used should dictate the types of information provided.

As indicated earlier, few agencies have actually contacted owners of infill land to determine whether the property is available for development or under what terms and conditions. Small communities with relatively few parcels may want to add more information on ownership to their parcel files (beyond name and address). This could include phone number, current plans for development (if any), anticipated availability, price or rent asked, and the name/location of the listing broker (if any). This can save time and effort for builders who might be interested in approaching vacant landowners. In cities with thousands of vacant parcels, contacting all owners would probably be infeasible. More importantly, because plans can change quickly, this information must be regularly updated.

Dissemination

If the objective in establishing a vacant parcel file system is to encourage development of vacant sites, it is important to consider how information is disseminated to real estate interests and community groups. Many cities fail to adequately publicize the availability of parcel file data. Printouts are kept in the planning department or at the economic development agency, and are available if developers want to look at them, but no active attempt is made to create interest in or to encourage use of the data. Although staff will respond promptly to requests for information, cities do not use their parcel files aggressively.

There are a few notable exceptions to this generalization. Dallas promotes use of its vacant land file and closely monitors requests for information from developers. The city makes information on vacant land within its block grant target areas available free of charge; for other sites, it charges for the cost of reproducing computer output. The District of Columbia has published an attractive brochure on its Municipal Automated Geographic Information System; the pamphlet has been extensively distributed to area realtors, developers, and public interest groups. Other cities provide lists of vacant lots in selected areas for distribution to neighborhood organizations.

Cities tend to become more actively involved in promoting the development of publicly owned lots. Catalogs or flyers describing available sites (sometimes with photographs or maps) are prepared and mailed to brokers and developers. Public auctions are vigorously advertised rather than merely listed in the legal notices of the local newspaper. Where permitted by law, agency staff have directly approached builders (both local and national) with proven expertise in handling infill sites regarding concepts/plans for specific parcels.

Examples of some of the more innovative parcel files are offered on the following pages. It should be noted that three of the five systems described cover developed as well as vacant lots and are used for a wide variety of planning purposes.

Objectives. To develop an effective support system for all participating agencies.

Data Sources. Assessor's tax file and digitized assessor's maps.

Coverage. All of Lane County (4,610 square miles).

Information Collected for Vacant Land.

Parcel file:
Digitized perimeters
Parcel centroid
Acreage
Zoning
Plan designation
Assessed value
Commonly used geocodes
  census tracts and block groups
  municipalities
  special districts
  soil types
  floodplain
Tax lot number

Other files include:
X/Y coordinates
Water lines
Sewer lines
Streets

Updating. Annual. Uses building permits as well as annual update of assessor's maps and property assessments. Parcel file is always at least one year out-of-date when it is released.

Costs. Five person years of work (included $50,000 from HUD and $30,000 from Lane Council of Governments and city of Eugene). Maintenance costs started at $55,000 a year and by 1982 will be up to $104,000 just for salaries.

Dissemination. Maps at any scale can be drawn by computer. Requests for information can be answered by staff using one of 350 terminals connected to the data base. System also can provide special reports.

Use by Elected Officials.
Internal planning reports
Location of new public facilities
Metropolitan plan update
Planning decisions

Use by Private Interests.
Special requests answered on
sales trends and land availability.

Contact.
Jim Carlson
Program Manager-Research
Lane Council of Governments
125 E. 8th Avenue
Eugene, Oregon 97401
(503) 687-4283

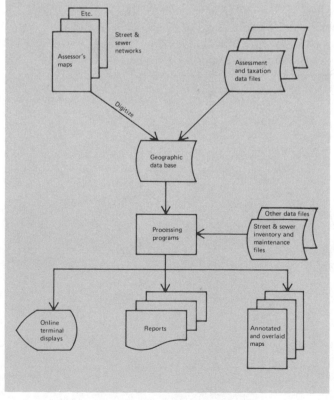

A model of the Lane County Geographic Data System.

Objectives. To keep track of vacant parcels.

Data Sources. Field survey and administrative records.

Coverage. Entire city of Wilmington. Also includes vacant buildings.

Information Collected for Vacant Land.
Owner's name and address
Last update of parcel records
Block condition (qualitative)*
Lot condition*
Perceived impact on neighborhood*
Feasible development for lots (new development or add-on to adjacent use)*
Lot dimensions
Zoning
Back taxes due
Planned city actions (acquisition or disposition)
Parcel tax number
Adjacent lots with same owner
Covers over 500 vacant lots and nearly 1,400 vacant buildings.

*These items are based on field inspections.

Updating. First published in 1979. Updated twice a year.

Costs. Six person months to create original inventory of privately owned vacant land. Six person months for the inventory of city-owned vacant land (these figures include time spent on inventorying vacant buildings as well). Total of 114 hours a month, for both files, to keep current. Use staff interns for updating.

Dissemination. Summaries are occasionally released.

Use by Elected Officials.
Public works planning and site selection for municipal facilities
Management of city-owned property
Licensing and inspection

Use by Private Interests. Vacant lot information provided to developers upon request.

Contact.
Gladys Spikes
Department of Real Estate and Housing
City of Wilmington
800 French Street
Wilmington, Delaware 19801
(302) 571-4057

Objectives. To identify residential development opportunities.

Data Sources. Vacant parcel file taken from assessor's tax rolls. Includes those parcels with no improvements.

Coverage. Entire city of Dallas. Does not include tax-exempt parcels.

Information Collected for Vacant Land.
Name of the taxpayer
Zoning
Front footage
Infrastructure (alleys and utilities—water, sewer, gas, and electricity)
Streets (improved or unimproved)
Geocoding
    Parcel address
    Census geography
    Legal description
    Community designation

Updating. Developed in 1979, first updated in 1980. Future updates to be prepared annually.

Costs. Information not available.

Dissemination. Computer printouts listing parcels by neighborhood are free for CDBG eligible areas. A charge of 20 cents per page is made for other areas.

Use by Elected Officials. Memos are provided to the city council with vacant parcel counts for the CDBG target area, as well as the balance of the city. Staff also respond to special requests.

Use by Private Interests. Some residential developers work with the city on site selection. Others use the printouts by themselves. The city feels that over 120 new housing units are directly attributable to the project. Additional units are under construction. City staff closely monitor the use of this information and work aggressively to provide developers with data on vacant sites.

Contact.
Judith Kovisars
Department of Housing and
  Urban Rehabilitation
Housing Research, Planning
  and Information Section
City Hall
1500 Marilla
Dallas, Texas 75201
(214) 670-3602

```
VACANT NON-TAX-EXEMPT LAND PARCELS IN CITY OF DALLAS   10/31/78
                                                        PAGE  4183
        CENSUS TRACT   1       COMMUNITY LAKEWOOD

###############################################################

PARCEL ADDRESS:          6801 CLAYTON AVE       75214
CENSUS GEOGRAPHY:        TRACT    1     BLOCK   306
LEGAL GEOGRAPHY:         LOT 006  BLOCK        A/2749
LEGAL DESCRIPTION:       PT 6 52.5X156
                         CLAYTON & BRENDENWOOD

TAXPAYER INFORMATION:    BEZIRIAN LELA RHEA
                         X FT WORTH MTG CO

ZONING:                  R75
LAND USE CODE:           9100
FRONTAGE(S):             53   FEET ON    CLAYTON AVE
                         156  FEET ON    BRENDENWOOD DR
UTILITIES PRESENT:       WATER SEWER GAS ELECTRICITY
STREET TYPE:             PERMANENT
                         WITH CURB AND GUTTERS

===============================================================
###############################################################

PARCEL ADDRESS:          6807 CLAYTON AVE       75214
CENSUS GEOGRAPHY:        TRACT    1     BLOCK   306
LEGAL GEOGRAPHY:         LOT 007  BLOCK        A/2749
LEGAL DESCRIPTION:       PT 7 26.25X156
                         CLAYTON 105FR BRENDENWOOD

TAXPAYER INFORMATION:    BEZIRIAN LELA RHEA
                         X FT WORTH MTG CO

ZONING:                  R75
LAND USE CODE:           9100
FRONTAGE(S):             26   FEET ON   CLAYTON AVE
UTILITIES PRESENT:       WATER SEWER GAS ELECTRICITY
STREET TYPE:             PERMANENT
                         WITH CURB AND GUTTERS

===============================================================
```

Computer printout of the vacant parcel file for Dallas, Texas.

Objectives. To provide a wide selection of current and accurate information needed by city staff and elected officials in their analysis of problems and potential changes in city services.

Data Sources.
Assessor's real estate file
Other city data files
Field checks

Coverage. All parcels in the city of Milwaukee. 160,000 parcels total (vacant and developed).

Information Collected for Vacant Land.

Tax key number	Aldermanic district
Street address	Indicator for corner lot
Current assessment	Lot size and area
Previous assessment	Code for tax-exempt properties
Date of change in value	Zoning
Date of change of owner	Land use code (one vacant category)
Owner's name and address	Census geocodes (tracts, blocks, block groups)

Updating. Three times a year from assessor's real estate file.

Costs. No estimates are available for the original file development. Updates use about $5,000 a year in computer resources, plus additional labor. Partially funded with CDBG money.

Dissemination. Data available at computer terminals for city officials. Summary documents and reports released to the public. Presentations made to neighborhood and community leaders. Special runs for neighborhood and community groups at cost, upon approval of department head.

Use by Private Interests. Special requests honored upon approval of department head; computer costs charged to the users.

Problems Encountered. Making sure that users understand the content of reports.

Contact.
William E. Huxhold
Project Director
Policy Development Information System
City of Milwaukee
783 North Water Street, Room 200
Milwaukee, Wisconsin 53202
(414) 278-3877

Objectives. Initially used to target areas for city programs.

Data Sources. Assessor's files and real estate information recorded by other District government departments (such as zoning).

Coverage. Entire District of Columbia—250,000 parcels in 105-square-mile area. Includes vacant and developed properties.

Information Collected for Vacant Land.
Parcel legal address
Owner's name and address
Lot size
Tax status
Zoning
Sales records since 1970
Vacant land identifier
Assessed value
Land ownership (private taxable, city, federal)
Geocodes:
  Census tracts and blocks
  Community areas
  Ward boundaries

Updating. Annual

Costs. $330,000 in CDBG funds to develop; $100,000 a year in maintenance costs.

Dissemination. A brochure describing the system is distributed to the public. Public interest groups use the data base for special studies. MAGIS can produce an outline of the city with different shadings to represent values in different census tracts or blocks.

Use by Elected Officials.
Targeting areas for public programs
Vacant land study conducted by city council staff
Special studies (e.g., downtown historic preservation, rehabilitation of vacant buildings for low- and moderate-income families, impact of subway stops on land values, and ownership holdings)

Use by Private Interests. Real estate brokers use the data.

Contact.
Konrad J. Perlman
District of Columbia
Department of Housing and
  Community Development
1133 North Capitol Street, N.E.
Washington, D.C. 20002
(202) 535-1245

Identifying Locations for Public Action

Larger cities lacking the resources to create areawide vacant land inventories or parcel files may want to focus their identification of infill opportunities on a limited number of target locations. This effort can also be useful in setting priorities for the more active forms of infill encouragement, such as capital improvement programs, land acquisition/assembly, or financial assistance. In identifying neighborhoods with infill potential, planning staff should be alert to areas:

- whose existing building stock has been well-maintained or where evidence of recent rehabilitation activity can be seen (either strictly private or publicly assisted).
- near strong central business districts, both urban and suburban, where employment is growing and amenities (shopping, cultural facilities, and recreation areas) are nearby. In many cities, such land was cleared in the 1960s and 1970s under urban renewal programs and is only now being sought by the private sector.
- with stable, moderate- to middle-income populations and businesses to serve them.
- with neighborhood organizations that support new investment and development.
- near existing suburban activity centers, such as regional shopping centers or office nodes.
- near existing industrial areas, where infill land can provide expansion space for existing manufacturers and warehouses or offer locational advantages for incubator businesses.
- surrounding or bordering anchor institutions (such as hospitals and universities) that employ large numbers of relatively well-paid professionals.
- with residential subdivisions or industrial parks that have not been fully built out. These projects may have suffered from escalating interest rates over the past two years. If the sites are not legally encumbered (i.e., due to bankruptcy of developers or other liens on title), they should be absorbed once real estate finance conditions become more normalized.

Not all neighborhoods will offer an attractive environment for infill building in the short run. Where existing structures have deteriorated, vacancies are high, and building values are low, new construction will not be feasible without public subsidies or heavy infusions of "sweat equity." While residents of such neighborhoods are eager to attract new investment, few developers will be willing to take the risk. However, these neighborhoods should not be ignored as cities formulate infill strategies. They are good candidates for demonstration programs (often involving locally based, nonprofit development corporations), land banking, and infrastructure upgrading.

For neighborhoods that appear to have potential, city staff should map and inspect vacant parcels, describe zoning provisions and physical characteristics, document location amenities, note parcel sizes and land assembly potential, and identify/contact property owners. These data can be used in preparing neighborhood plans and reviewing them with local residents and elected officials. Once agreement is reached on an overall strategy, the city can prepare promotional materials and technical reports for distribution to brokers and builders. In addition to site-specific information, these reports should contain general background on the neighborhood:

- major employers, numbers of business establishments, goods and services offered.
- anchor institutions and their plans for growth.
- trends in population and household formation.
- income characteristics of residents.
- transportation access.
- descriptions and illustrations of recent investment activity (infilling, rehabilitation, redevelopment) for a variety of land uses and project sizes. Marketing success should be prominently featured.
- sales prices/values of existing homes.
- rents paid in existing Class A commercial space.

Promoting Uniquely Attractive Sites

Not all cities will want to "market" their infill sites on a neighborhood basis. They may prefer to promote specific properties that offer unique opportunities for large-scale development. These properties might include:

- large tracts assembled through earlier urban renewal efforts for which market conditions have improved.
- underutilized properties owned by railroads, foundations, or religious orders and no longer needed by these owners.
- surplus federal or state-owned land, such as that occupied by military installations scheduled for closing or obsolete correctional facilities.
- golf courses and country clubs that are no longer in operation.
- land near airports, new expressways, rail spurs, upgraded arterials, transit stations, and modernized port facilities.
- sites with access to rivers or lake shores. Many cities are making progress in reducing waterway pollution. Public investment in cleanup and amenities can be directed toward promising vacant properties.
- properties near tourist attractions and within historic districts. The character of development will have to blend harmoniously with existing building styles and densities.

Projects in these locations may require clearance and redevelopment as well as infilling on land already vacant.

Encouraging Infill Development

In most cities and older suburbs, local government actually can assist infill efforts—either citywide, in a few target neighborhoods, or for individual projects. Such actions need not involve the creation of expensive new government programs or extensive new demands on local staff. Rather, government involvement in infilling will require better targeting of existing resources as part of a city's development strategy.

The examples of city and state programs included here focus largely on incentives to improve infill development feasibility and make infilling competitive with suburban fringe development. They deal with infill housing and do not deal specifically with commercial and industrial uses. While not ignoring larger projects—which can contribute significantly to urban and suburban revitalization—special attention is given to the problems encountered with small-scale infilling. Small projects are subject to many problems: costly code provisions, procedural delays, neighborhood opposition, recalcitrant landowners, weak or uncertain market conditions, and high land prices. They are not as appealing to local officials as large-scale projects—and do not receive as much special attention—because individual small projects do not, in and of themselves, contribute much to the city's tax base or revitalization efforts. In the aggregate, though, they can have a major impact in addressing urban problems while providing greater housing and business opportunities.

Many of these incentives are not "new"; they have been used by various cities and counties for many years as part of their overall community development efforts. They have been applied to redevelopment, rehabilitation, and adaptive use, as well as infilling. Figure 3-1 lists the types of incentives described in this chapter and the cities and counties used as illustrative examples.

Stimulating Developer Interest In Infilling

Generating awareness of opportunities is a fundamental first step in encouraging infill development activity. Builders and developers should be encouraged to use city vacant land inventories, parcel files, and infill incentive programs. Planning and development staff should attend meetings of local builder/realtor organizations to present information on infill opportunities. Publicity efforts can include a slide show and written materials on representative sites, along with sample project financial analyses to indicate the potential profits associated with project development. City incentives for infilling can be described. Colorado Springs is one city that is effectively using seminars and meetings to acquaint real estate interests with infill potential. Omaha informs builders annually about shifting development trends and city infill incentives.

For architects and builders with little or no infill experience, design competitions can offer an inexpensive way to heighten awareness of the development potential of small or oddly shaped sites. At the same time, competitions foster better quality infill designs that are more compatible with existing housing and therefore more likely to win the support of nearby property owners. Prize money can be awarded within different categories—single-family and multifamily housing, offices, convenience retailing and service business, and site planning for small subdivisions. Local foundations may be willing to provide the prize money, and the awards can be published in the local press and in professional journals. The cost to the city is fairly low; it requires staff time in identifying representative sites, soliciting prize money and jurors, and handling publicity. Such programs have recently been sponsored by the city of St. Paul and a neighborhood-based housing development corporation in Chicago (in cooperation with the local chapter of the American Institute of Architects). Some of the competitions have focused on sites with peculiar physical or environmental problems. In New Jersey a state-sponsored effort focused on low-cost designs suitable for families earning $15,000 or less. Local housing authorities, as well as private firms, were able to participate.

Another approach is for cities to publish a pamphlet or brochure showing sketch plans, layouts, and photographs of attractive examples of infilling that have already been built in various locations. The examples should depict a variety of project scales, densities, and styles, focusing on how small sites can be effectively used in harmony with surrounding older structures.

Figure 3-1
What Local Governments Can Do

Section	Contents	Examples
Stimulate Developer Interest in Infilling	• Publicity campaigns and meetings with real estate interests • Design competitions	• Colorado Springs, CO • Omaha, NB • State of New Jersey • St. Paul, MN • Minneapolis, MN
Remove Obstacles Created by Government	• Reduce delays in project review • Code revisions	• Kansas City, MO • Livermore, CA • Winston-Salem, NC • Colorado Springs, CO • Seattle, WA • Montgomery County, MD • Omaha, NB • Modesto, CA • Portland, OR • Phoenix, AZ
Create Neighborhood Support for Infilling	• Review meetings • Special procedures • Area targeting	• Baltimore, MD • Minneapolis, MN • Phoenix, AZ
Address Market Weakness or Uncertainty	• Lower risk • Advantageous financing • Demonstration projects • Maintenance and rehabilitation • Service upgrading • Interim uses	• Dallas, TX • Minneapolis/St. Paul, MN • Los Angeles, CA • Birmingham, AL • Springfield, IL • Chicago, IL • Bronx, NY • Oakland, CA • New York, NY • Wilmington, DE
Address Site Specific Problems	• Increase land availability • Reduce the high cost of land and improvements • Correct infrastructure problems	• San Diego, CA • Portland, OR • Polk County, IA • San Mateo County, CA • Duluth, MN • Phoenix, AZ • Omaha, NB • Baltimore, MD • New York, NY
Increase Land Availability	• Eminent domain • Land swapping • Tax vacant land at higher rates • Land banking	• St. Louis, MO • Omaha, NB
Combine Infill Incentives in Effective Strategies	• Package tools and techniques • Use state and federal assistance	

Objectives. To indicate visually the physical and service constraints, or lack thereof, of vacant lands. Also to facilitate development of those vacant lands by expediting city council, city planning commission, and general public approval through the use of the map series.

Description. The city has identified all developable vacant land and put together a series of approximately 20 base maps that display the infrastructure system—streets, wastewater, transit system, land use relationships, water lines, electrical lines, police patrol patterns, fire response time, and school district capacities. Data from each base map is transferred to a clear acetate overlay so that any combination of overlays can be used to quickly determine a site's characteristics. The map series has been designed so that the vacant land is discernible with the entire series of infrastructure overlays in place.

Accomplishments. Reactions to the map series have been very positive. The series is used regularly by developers, city council, and the Chamber of Commerce. In addition, the planning department has assumed the role of educator and has given speeches to a wide variety of groups (e.g., Home Builders Association, Landmarks Council, League of Women Voters, service organizations, environmental groups) on the benefits of the map series. There have also been newspaper articles and television coverage on the maps and the need for infill in Colorado Springs.

Costs. The map series cost about $4,000–$5,000, including $500 for materials. It took a city planner and a skilled draftsman approximately four months to prepare the series. This does not include the cost of original inventory preparation.

Areas Covered. The city has a vigorous annexation policy. Within the city limits, 42 percent of the land is vacant. The map series covers all vacant land that is developable.

Contact.
Bud Owsley
Director of Planning
City Hall
Box 1575
Colorado Springs, Colorado 80901
(303) 471-6868

Objectives. To provide information on growth patterns, in order to determine whether adjustments should be made to the city of Omaha's adopted growth management system, the "Urban Development Policy."

Description. Since 1977 Omaha has compiled an annual growth monitoring report. The report includes statistics on both inner-city and outlying building permits, lot availability, land availability, absorption rates, and home values. Keeping close track of actual patterns of growth and development allows the city to make the best use of its resources.

Accomplishments. By keeping close tabs on development trends in the various portions of the Omaha jurisdiction (municipal plus three-mile extraterritorial), Omaha has identified subtle changes in the market. For example, one suburban infill area had maintained a negative development image during the early- to mid-1970s, due in part to court-ordered busing in the school district for that sector. However, the statistics showed certain potentially positive trends by 1978, and the development community was made more aware of these changes through the publication of this report. Today, development rates in this sector closely parallel those in other suburban areas.

Constraints. Developers are increasingly interested in detailed information, while this report provides only totals for large subareas of the city and suburbs.

Costs. Taken as a whole, the activity costs the city about $10,000 a year, with approximately 80 percent going to staff salaries and 20 percent to data processing, aerial photography, and the like. About 10 percent of the funding is from CDBG funds.

Contact.
Susan Ruby
City Planning Department
City of Omaha
1819 Farnam Street
Omaha, Nebraska 68183
(402) 444-5217

Objectives. The construction of three basic one- or two-family houses that might serve as prototypes.

Description. The competition was held in two stages: (1) a design stage and (2) a construction and marketing stage. The competition was open to individuals or teams that had some expertise in the field of housing and qualified as New Jersey residents. The design package was to include a sound financing plan and be affordable for a cross-section of moderate-income families. A panel of judges (representing the private banking industry, public agencies, private organizations involved in modest-cost housing, and the planning and architectural community) was selected to review entries and award prizes. The first stage called for a single-family or two-family house design and cost estimate suitable for submission to a financial institution for mortgage commitment. Exhibits of winning entries from the first stage were displayed at various locations around the state to stimulate public exposure and response. The second stage entailed the actual construction and marketing of the affordable house.

Accomplishments. The competition focused statewide attention on the need for new housing alternatives for moderate-income urbanites. It stimulated innovative designs for low-cost, quality housing. The program also caused public officials to realize the advantages of utilizing tax-foreclosed land for infill housing development. The Housing Authority of Bergen County purchased sites for construction of 10 additional duplex units of the type winning a Phase I award. This is an ongoing program utilizing $1 million in HUD money for land banking purposes.

Costs. The total prize money, which amounted to $11,000, was supplied by the New Jersey Department of Community Affairs through its Housing Demonstration Grant Fund. Three awards of $2,000 each were given for the initial stage of the competition. A grand prize of $5,000 was awarded for the second stage of construction and marketing for the single best solution to housing moderate-income families in urban infill situations. Construction cost for the two-family homes was $69,000 to $80,000, excluding land. Lot prices ranged from $16,000 to $40,000. Site acquisition subsidies from the land bank program ranged from $4,000 to $20,000. All units were sold for approximately $40,000.

Eligible Locations/Targeting. Any location within the state. Home was to be affordable by families earning under $15,000.

Contact.
Jerome Shaw
New Jersey Department
  of Community Affairs
363 N. State Street
Trenton, New Jersey 08625
(609) 292-0508

Objectives. The objective of the design competition was to encourage, by example, livable, small-scale infill architecture that could work next to some of the city's older housing structures.

Description. In an attempt to encourage high quality, small-scale single-family design, St. Paul's Department of Planning and Economic Development sponsored an urban design competition in the summer of 1979. The city made available eight city inventory lots, none exceeding 40 feet in width. Over 70 contestants designed housing to fit on one of the city's lots. Contestants were judged on their design's solution to the limited space issue, energy efficiency, and aesthetic compatibility with surrounding structures.
After initial submissions were made, the second phase of the competition entailed selecting five semifinalists who each received $500. Of these, three finalists were given $2,500 and a city lot to actually construct the home they had designed. Low-interest financing was provided through the city's below-market interest rate mortgage bond program. The house was displayed to the general public after construction.

Accomplishments. The project generated considerable response: over 70 contestants entered. For future reference, the city compiled an inventory of those contestants whose designs were most successful.

Costs and Funding. The entire project cost the city $15,000, which was obtained from CDBG funds.

Eligible Locations. All of the city's subject lots were located in the university and Frogtown neighborhoods. These blue-collar neighborhoods house low- to moderate-income persons but have very low unemployment rates. According to the city, these neighborhoods deteriorated in the past but now are in the process of resurgence.

Contacts.
Bill Pearson or Shannon Kelley
St. Paul Department of Planning and Economic Development
City Hall Annex
25 W. 4th Street
St. Paul, Minnesota 55102
(612) 292-6720

Objectives. To prove that earth-sheltered, multi-dwelling-unit housing could be attractive and marketable in a marginal location that bordered a noisy freeway.

Description. In an effort to retain an underutilized land parcel for housing, Seward West Redesign, Inc., a nonprofit neighborhood organization, proposed to build attractive solar row housing to replace 11 deteriorated single-family units. Six of the original houses were demolished and the remaining five moved and rehabilitated within the area. Seward West received grants from the Department of Energy for the solar heating system, and procured interest-free loans and grant monies from local sources. The project began in the fall of 1978 and was completed in the spring of 1979.

Accomplishments. Every unit was sold within a year of construction. Tremendous interest was also generated in the hybrid solar feature of the house. Thousands of people attended the six-month open house after construction.

Costs. Grants for the solar system were provided by the Department of Energy and Department of Housing and Urban Development. Other grants and noninterest loans were provided by the Minnesota Housing Finance Agency (MHFA), Control Data Corporation, and the Greater Metropolitan Housing Corporation, while CDBG funds financed the development of the site.
Eleven units were sold for the following prices:
    2 BR (1,058 sq. ft.) = $70,000
    2 BR (1,275 sq. ft.) = $80,000
The 12th unit was sold for the subsidized price of $48,300 through the MHFA innovative housing program.

Contact.
Seward West Redesign, Inc.
(612) 338-1664

Michael Dunn
Close Associates (Architects)
3101 East Franklin
Minneapolis, Minnesota 55406
(612) 339-0979

Solar and earth-sheltered row housing in Minneapolis.

Removing Obstacles Created by Government

Improving both local regulations and their administration can help to make infill development more appealing vis-a-vis fringe projects. A recent HUD publication, *Streamlining Land Use Regulation: A Guidebook for Local Governments*, offers many helpful suggestions for dealing with project review. Regulatory risk—the uncertainty associated with protracted development review procedures—is cited as an important factor in many developers' decisions to bypass sites within urbanized areas in favor of urban fringe locations. The authors cite market conditions and land prices as the primary motives behind leapfrogging, but indicate that regulatory delay can tip the scales. Complex permit systems discourage construction firms from working in locations where they have not worked before. Small builders simply cannot afford the holding costs or the legal and engineering fees required to gain needed approvals. Relatively inexperienced entrepreneurs can benefit most from procedural streamlining.

Figure 3-2 presents a summary list of procedural reforms suggested by HUD-sponsored research. Many of these suggestions are applicable to large and small projects, redevelopment or rehabilitation, as well as to infilling. Cities that want to improve their competitive position and to maintain low costs would do well to consider these recommendations. While not easy to implement politically or administratively, procedural reform can be a fairly low-cost way of improving infill feasibility.

State governments can also help to remove regulatory roadblocks. For example, the California legislature is considering exempting infill projects from reviews mandated under the California Environmental Quality Act. Cities have experimented with areawide environmental impact statements that could cover more than one project in a given neighborhood.

Excessively High or Inappropriate Standards

Problems peculiar to small-scale infilling often occur because today's development standards are inappropriate for lots platted 30 or 40 years ago. Development of lots that do not meet current size minimums requires a variance, which usually means a public hearing. Some cities allow lots platted under earlier standards to be "grandfathered" in; others are developing special review procedures for expediting minor exceptions to lot sizes, side and rear yard requirements, parking design, etc. Portland, Oregon, is one jurisdiction that has paid particular attention to the problem of substandard lots. Omaha has reduced its setback requirements in certain single-family zones to allow greater site coverage.

Current standards may not be appropriate for the types of attached single-family housing that can efficiently use small infill spaces (duplexes, townhouses, zero lot line, cluster techniques). Some jurisdictions, such as King County, Washington, and Montgomery County, Maryland, are adopting special townhouse or cluster zoning provisions for infill lots that meet defined criteria. Building codes are being modified to permit factory-built housing, which can be more efficient and economical for small, scattered construction projects than conventional construction techniques. Other cities are comprehensively reexamining and modifying their codes to reflect current planning practice, but this is a lengthy, expensive procedure that is often resisted by the bureaucracy, citizens, building trade unions, or real estate interests.

Zoning Balance

Another often-cited obstacle to infilling is government's failure to match the relative quantities of vacant land zoned for various uses and intensities with the probable demand for housing and nonresidential space over the next 10 to 20 years. Much has been said about large lot single-family zoning, the absence of adequate land supply for attached housing styles, or overzoning for commercial or industrial use. One or more of these problems exists in virtually every city, but they are not easy to correct. Owners of property zoned for commercial or industrial uses resist downzoning; neighborhood residents resist upzoning from single-family to multifamily designations. Comprehensive analyses of land supply and demand by zoning category can drain staff resources and will be accurate for only a short period of time. Attention should first be focused on locations with the most obviously inappropriate designations (i.e., land zoned industrial in locations distant from transportation access or parcels zoned for single-family use scattered in the midst of strip commercial development).

Figure 3-2
Techniques for Streamlining Land Use Regulation

Preapplication Stage

- written materials (design manuals, developers' handbook)
- informal preapplication meetings
- centralized information and permit counters

Staff Review Stage

- interdepartmental review committees
- fast tracking project with minor impacts
- simultaneous review of multiple permits
- master environmental impact reports
- mandatory review time frames
- permit expeditors or ombudsmen
- departmental reorganization
- improved information systems

Lay Review Stage

- training for review board members
- reducing public hearing backlogs (more frequent meetings)
- improving hearing procedures
- informal meetings with neighborhood organizations
- consolidating or eliminating multiple hearings
- redefining planning commission roles
- using a hearing examiner
- creating dual planning commissions
- mediating of disputes

Source: U.S. Department of Housing and Urban Development. Office of Policy Development and Research, *Streamlining Land Use Regulation: A Guidebook for Local Governments*, November 1980.

Objectives. The stated objectives of Kansas City's ordinance are to lessen the time required to review and to process development proposals, to lower the requirements for both large- and small-scale developments, and to provide greater specificity in city development requirements.

Description. Kansas City adopted a new land use and development code in November 1980. The code is an addition to the zoning ordinance, and its purpose is to expedite the review procedures on development proposals and to clarify contradictions in the zoning ordinance. Also, developers do not have to submit as much material as was once required by the zoning and planning commission.

Accomplishments. The changes were only recently adopted; it is too early to identify accomplishments.

Constraints. There was no real opposition to the code. In fact, it was well received by city officials and the real estate community.

Eligible Locations. The code is effective on a citywide basis. At this point, no targeting has been attempted.

Contact.
Bill Hartman
Kansas City Development Department
City Hall - 15th Floor
414 East 12th Street
Kansas City, Missouri 64106
(816) 274-1844

Objectives. To encourage close-in development.

Description. Livermore's Residential Development Plan allows a two percent maximum annual growth in the number of housing units. Limited sewer capacity prevents a higher rate of expansion. The 360 sewer permits available annually are awarded to developers based on a point system. Proposed projects surrounded by existing development receive more points than those in the outlying district of the city. (Points are also given for design quality, energy efficiency, housing mix, and provision of major public facilities.) The point system is a method that allows developers to bid for development rights.

Accomplishments. No hard figures are available on the impact of the program on developer activities. The Livermore city manager's office feels that it has been relatively "successful in forcing contiguous development rather than leapfrogging projects."

Eligible Locations. A maximum of 200 points (of a total of 1,065 possible for development elements) can be given for project location, depending on the area of the general plan in which the project falls. In the short-range area, projects received two points for every percentage of the project site that joins with existing developed areas; in the medium-range area, one point is given for every percentage; and in the long-range area, 0.5 point. Lots of record allowing for four or fewer units are exempt from the plan's process.

Costs. Cannot be isolated from other development processing/review expenditures.

Contact.
Barbara Hempill
Office of the City Manager
1052 S. Livermore Avenue
Livermore, California 94550
(415) 449-4000

Objectives. To provide ideas for developers who are unsure of best use options for a particular urban parcel and to assist in providing more efficient use of infill land.

Description. The Forsyth County and Winston-Salem City-County Planning Board offer site design assistance to interested developers. Also, to increase residential densities for vacant sites, the Board is more flexible in granting density zoning amendments when they will encourage infill development. The Planned Residential District (PRD) designation and special use district zoning have been the most effective tools in this regard.

Eligible Locations. All areas under the board's jurisdiction are eligible for the above services.

Constraints. The only opposition to both tools is the resistance that some property owners display when higher densities are allowed to enter their neighborhoods.

Costs. The design assistance occupies such a small part of the planning board design staff's time that the cost, in terms of staff person hours, is negligible.

Accomplishments. It is impossible to quantify the amount of infilling resulting from design assistance. However, in combination with the PRD option and special use district zoning, design assistance has several times defused opposition to rezoning for higher density development.

Contact.
Harry Weiler
Senior Planner
City-County Planning Board of Forsyth County and Winston-Salem
P.O. Box 2511
Winston-Salem, North Carolina 27102
(919) 727-2548

Objectives. To provide a thorough representation of the positive and negative aspects of infill development proposals. Avoids controversy in later public hearings.

Description. When proposals are presented for a master plan change, new subdivision change, or zoning change, the planning department routes a comment sheet (or buck slip) to other city department staff. Each sheet is specifically tailored for each department and requires responses in measurable units. The idea behind the sheet is to ensure that potential problem areas are identified as early as possible and subsequently resolved in an effort to help facilitate infill development. Approximately 10 sheets will be created to indicate the effect of the proposed project on:
- utilities (gas, water, electric, wastewater)
- public works
- fire and police protection
- community development/land use
- parks and recreation

After each department has responded, the planning department prepares a summary matrix and a final report to the city planning commission.

Accomplishments. The planning department is presently refining the process and formats. To date, it has not been used as a key determinant in city council approval. However, it has proved to be a means of increasing communication between developers and the planning department at an early stage of development.

Constraints. Because the process requires thorough and comprehensive review of the impacts of infill projects, it can be time consuming.

Costs. No costs can be directly attributable to this procedure as distinct from other review procedures.

Eligible Locations. The original purpose of the procedure was to focus on infill projects throughout the city. However, it could be used for all types of development and has been tested on two other types: an annexation request of an enclave and a master plan for a new development outside the city limits.

Contact.
Bud Owsley
Director of Planning
City Hall
Box 1575
Colorado Springs, Colorado 80901
(303) 471-6868

Objectives. To encourage new housing construction, while preserving existing neighborhood character.

Description. New policies eliminate density limits, lot coverage requirements, and minimum lot size regulations to make it easier to build infill housing on small lots. By paying more attention to appearance—and stripping away some traditional zoning restrictions—Seattle has increased its capacity for housing while downzoning some areas to single-family and reducing height in areas formerly zoned for high-rises. The policies make possible a decrease in overall production costs of $1,500 to $1,700 per unit for townhouses and apartments through modest increases in density on small lots. The policies provide incentives for townhouses, duplexes, and apartments with private ground level open space. The method for measuring height has been changed to better reflect topography and preserve views. The design of off-street parking and the width of apartment buildings are strictly regulated. There is no restriction on the number of units per lot area. An administrative procedure called "design departure" eliminates much of the need for zoning variances and encourages good design.

Constraints. While a coalition of neighborhood preservationists, housing advocates, architects, and the housing industry supported the policies, no one was totally satisfied. Local preferences for single-family detached housing resulted in the downzoning of substantial acreage to single-family status. Proposals for new high-rise areas were defeated. There is concern over displacement because of the increased pressure to demolish older houses in multifamily zones.

Costs. Information not available.

Eligible Locations. All multifamily land in the city. Seattle is overhauling its zoning starting with residential areas, then commercial areas and downtown, and finally industrial areas and open spaces.

Contact.
Beatrice Ryan
Manager, Special Projects
Office of Policy and Evaluation
City of Seattle
303 Municipal Building
Seattle, Washington 98104
(206) 625-4591

Objectives. To permit more attractive and economically feasible development of passed-over vacant sites. Many of these sites are substantially smaller than the minimum 10 acres previously required for cluster development.

Description. In order to permit residential cluster development (detached, semidetached, and townhouse units) to occur, a zoning text amendment was adopted by the county council, permitting lot sizes to be reduced and site layout specifications to be more flexible. The program requires submission of site plans to the planning board, in addition to review by community and other public bodies prior to approval. The ordinance was adopted in 1978.

Accomplishments. The cluster development amendment has resulted in a number of private developments throughout Montgomery County.

Costs. The program does not generate any discernible costs to the local government. All site development costs are paid by the developer.

Eligible Locations. All areas under the jurisdiction of the planning commission are eligible for the smaller lot requirements for residential cluster developments. However, its primary impact is in the more heavily developed areas closest to the District of Columbia.

Contact.
E. Lael Adams
Principal Planner
The Maryland-National Capital Park and Planning Commission
8787 Georgia Avenue
Silver Spring, Maryland 20907
(301) 565-7355

Objectives. To encourage infill development on skipped-over parcels by allowing cost-reducing design options.

Description. In 1979, the city created a new zoning category (R5A), which allowed single-family homes to be built 10 feet closer to the street right of way. Approximately 20 percent of the 600 to 800 single-family lots platted each year are now zoned R5A, allowing an estimated $500–$1,000 savings per unit. More recently, lot splits for duplex construction have also been permitted (R6) allowing (in effect) zero lot line housing with independent lot ownership of each half.

Accomplishments. The program's accomplishments are difficult to establish. The R6 change was implemented only a few months ago; the time elapsed is not sufficient to document its impact. There have been several small subdivisions constructed in the inner city.

Constraints. The R5A zoning was supported by all developers. There is occasional opposition by neighbors of specific projects when they believe that setback aesthetics are being violated.

Eligible Locations. The change is citywide, but it allows use of more skipped-over land in closer-in neighborhoods.

Costs. Research and implementation required minimal staff time. Administration is nominal.

Contact.
Blythe Kubovac
Board of Appeals
City of Omaha
1819 Farnam
Omaha, Nebraska 68183
(402) 444-5210

Objectives. To enhance efficiency of provision of urban services through increased residential density and infilling of the urban area. Also, to preserve agricultural land.

Description. In 1974, the city council initiated a growth review process in order to balance housing needs against the available land inventory. Growth on the urban fringe was restricted by limiting sanitary sewer trunk extensions. A general plan change was adopted that allowed up to 10 units per net acre under planned development zoning in areas that would otherwise qualify for only 6.5 units per acre. Zoning code revisions were subsequently adopted in 1978 and 1980 to allow construction of duplexes on all corner lots in new R-1 (single-family) subdivisions, and reduce minimum lot size in the R-1 zone from 6,000 square feet to 5,000 square feet. The revision also permitted "flag" lots in R-1 zones, allowing maximum development on bypassed parcels with sufficient total area but narrow frontages.

Accomplishments. Modesto's overall residential density increased from 6.95 units per acre in 1977 to 7.24 units per acre by 1980. From 75 to 100 projects have been constructed on R-1-zoned parcels since initiation of the code revisions. The planned development zoning (for patio homes and apartments) has accounted for most of the development in Modesto in the last few years.

Constraints. Opposition to the code revision was minimal. Concerns were voiced by property owners over anticipated problems with increased densities (i.e., noise, increased traffic flow, etc.).

Costs. The city experiences no real costs as a result of the revisions. Existing city infrastructure is able to accommodate the increased densities and demands upon city services.

Eligible Locations. Entire city of Modesto.

Contact.
George Osner
Associate Planner
City of Modesto Department of Planning and Community Development
801 Eleventh
P.O. Box 642
Modesto, California 95353
(209) 577-5275

Objectives. To provide additional inner city land for development, to encourage greater urban densities, and to reduce the number of zoning variance requests.

Description. Most of Portland has historically been platted into 5,000-square-foot lots of 50 ft. × 100 ft. although whole neighborhoods have been platted with smaller frontages. In 1959, the 50 ft. × 100 ft. lot was declared the minimum size which could be developed by right. A 1978 study showed that of roughly 4,770 vacant substandard lots in the city, over half were at least 70 percent of the standard size. Moreover, 30 percent to 50 percent of all zoning variance requests each year were for lot size variances. Consequently, the zoning code was revised to allow development by right of lots of at least 3,750 square feet (35 ft. × 80 ft.) platted before July 1, 1959; creation of new substandard lots is not allowed. At the same time, a new rowhouse zone with a 2,500-square-foot average and an 1,800-square-foot minimum was created to allow attached housing in carefully selected areas. Previously, all single-family zoning had been geared to detached units with side yards.

Accomplishments. Substandard lot development has increased, and attitudes toward granting variances for density have relaxed. Exact numbers of new units produced have not been tracked because substandard lots are now developed by right and go through the building department rather than the zoning board.

Costs. This code revision was a very small element of the total activity involved in adoption of Portland's first comprehensive plan. The plan necessitated other, more major zoning changes. The cost of the substandard lot activity is an insignificant portion of this larger project.

Contact.
Frank Frost
Chief Planner, Code Administration
City of Portland
612 S.W. Adler
Portland, Oregon 97205
(503) 248-4250

Objectives. To encourage infill development, density incentives are offered. The city describes the program as a two-year "special offer" on central area density allowances.

Description. Two increases in allowable density have been authorized by the city council for a period of two years:
- *"Automatic High-Rise."* In the central core of the city, where additional high-rise development is considered desirable, any development that includes residential units is automatically granted high-rise zoning. This will save developers the two to three months that are normally required to obtain a variance.
- *"Double Density."* In the "infill incentive area," or double density area, any multifamily-zoned area is eligible for very substantial density bonuses.

Eligible Areas. The automatic high-rise area includes the CBD and other parts of the city core totaling approximately three square miles. The infill incentive area, which surrounds it, is a seven- to 10-square-mile portion of central Phoenix.

Contact.
Richard Counts
Planning Director
City of Phoenix
251 West Washington
Phoenix, Arizona 85003
(602) 262-6364

Creating Neighborhood Support for Infilling

A city that wants to encourage infill should take an active role in anticipating and mediating disputes between developers and neighbors. Most cities lack an effective neighborhood planning process. Rarely are there small area plans that specify appropriate development options for individual vacant parcels. Confronting this controversial issue can help diffuse project-by-project bickering, and it can lead to demonstration of compatible design solutions and appropriate modifications in zoning and other standards.

City officials should also encourage more direct dialogue between development interests and community residents. As one Omaha developer noted, the secret is working with neighbors on the front end and being involved in neighborhood improvement efforts. Some communities, such as Baltimore, encourage early meetings between developers and local residents and businesspersons. Minneapolis requires meetings for larger apartment projects and townhouses. Developers will find that low-key private meetings prior to public hearings can result in increased popular support for their projects. When working in a given city or suburban neighborhood for the first time, they will be unfamiliar with neighborhood groups or uncertain about which ones are most important. City staff can be helpful in directing builders to the appropriate people. The concepts must then be properly presented, and the developer must be willing to listen to concerns and make reasonable modifications.

Planning staff should be certain that infill proposals are carefully (but promptly) reviewed and that potential problems are identified early before they meet opposition from neighborhoods or elected officials. Colorado Springs' detailed review checklists cover major environmental and public service capacity issues. Implementation of such procedures requires cooperation from many departments and can increase processing time, but it also identifies potential problems early so that they can be addressed by the developer before official hearings are held.

Objectives. To improve planning and design processes, to ensure compliance with the comprehensive plan, and to provide for early dialogue between builders and neighbors.

Description. This is really two programs: one for townhouses and one for multifamily, considered 10 or more units. Programs involve preliminary design review, and for the larger buildings, a neighborhood meeting conducted as a public hearing. A building permit is issued only if the final plan agrees with the approved concept plan.

Accomplishments. The plan review has been in effect for apartments since late 1975. The city reviews 10 to 12 projects a year under this plan. Few townhouse projects had been proposed in the city until recently. Relatively few have been reviewed under this process thus far. The recommendations have encouraged improvements in the project designs.

Constraints. Developers are not compelled to go along with recommendations that come out of the staff review or the hearing process. Court cases can arise.

Costs. Totally integrated within the planning department budget so costs of the additional review process cannot be isolated.

Eligible Locations. Entire city of Minneapolis.

Contact.
Michael Cronin
Development Controls Program
Minneapolis Planning Department
210 City Hall
Minneapolis, Minnesota 55415
(612) 348-2587

Objectives. To match more closely the requirements of developers with the wishes of the community.

Description. For the last 10 years, Baltimore has encouraged developers to hold preliminary meetings with community organizations before the details of a proposed development have been finalized. For projects involving city-owned land and in urban renewal areas, this is a requirement.

Accomplishments. Informal and formal agreements between developers and community organizations ensure community acceptance of developments. This prevents potential long delays in the formal filing process and official hearings. Potential conflict is averted. Developers of projects "of consequence" hold these meetings in virtually all instances.

Costs. No direct costs. Staff time is spent on the front end, working with developers and community groups. This time would otherwise be needed at later stages in the approval process.

Eligible Locations. Any developer can use this procedure throughout the city.

Contact.
Mark Sissman
City of Baltimore
Department of Housing and Community Development
222 East Saratoga
Baltimore, Maryland 21202
(301) 396-1965

Objectives. To provide neighborhoods with more latitude and a larger arsenal of tools to enhance their own development and vitality.

Description. Neighborhoods in Phoenix may seek designation as special conservation districts. The process of establishing a district is begun by petition of 30 percent of the property owners. After designation by the planning commission, districts are allowed to modify regulatory restrictions on development (e.g., zoning, setback requirements, and the like) in a way calculated to encourage development or to otherwise enhance the neighborhood. Actual modifications undertaken would depend to a large extent on local intent in establishing the district. Infill development would be the main objective in center city neighborhoods with large numbers of vacant or underutilized lots, whereas in other areas historic preservation or expansion of green space may be considered more urgent.

Accomplishments. Three special districts have been established to date. All are recent creations and thus have had no time to build records of accomplishments.

Constraints. The city reports no problems as yet with the new program besides the usual neighborhood scepticism. Because virtually no regulatory changes have yet been tested, it is too early to tell what difficulties such a program might entail.

Costs. Development of this program took an estimated three person months of staff time at the long range planning section of the city's neighborhood program.

Contact.
Richard F. Counts
Planning Director
251 W. Washington
Phoenix, Arizona 85003
(602) 262-6364

Addressing Market Weakness or Uncertainty

There are many older cities whose infill land supply is concentrated—in both scattered parcels and sizable tracts—in low-income areas. These cities are working to make such neighborhoods more attractive for private investment. Utilities and roads are being upgraded and police patrols and garbage collection services are being strengthened. Yet little or no private investor interest has surfaced. Because incomes and existing building values are low, few private developers are interested in constructing new housing in these neighborhoods in the absence of subsidies. Few lenders are willing to finance such high risk projects—especially when there are alternative opportunities available that offer the promise of greater return. New industrial development may be opposed by neighbors or may be of no interest to employers who worry about attracting and retaining a suitable labor force.

City actions alone usually cannot reverse years of declining maintenance, nor can they deal with inadequate purchasing power. Nevertheless, cities should continue to target their efforts in these neighborhoods in order to improve the development environment and stimulate private investment. This means not only bettering city services but also encouraging private maintenance and rehabilitation of existing buildings. Land banking of tax delinquent parcels can be a useful tool in assembling large tracts for redevelopment. These large-scale efforts will be most effective in turning around weak market areas. Offering city-owned land at little or no cost can also dramatically affect project feasibility by lowering prices or rents so that they are affordable for moderate-income households and the businesses that serve them.

Methods for Lowering Risk

Cities can help lower the risk in areas with image problems but otherwise attractive locations. A well-publicized example is Dallas's Bryan Place, a development of zero lot line houses that will eventually cover approximately 80 acres and provide 500 units for middle- and upper-income households in an area within walking distance of the CBD and the Baylor University medical center. Working with one of the nation's largest suburban homebuilders, the city of Dallas agreed to repurchase at cost (after a specified time period) any of the privately assembled land that could not be marketed. The project is now under way; initial phases have been very successful. Similar incentives have been available since 1975 for any residential development within two miles of the CBD.

Providing Advantageous Financing

Offering construction or permanent financing at below-market-interest rates can be extremely effective in attracting developers of income properties, home purchasers, or industrial users to infill sites. States, cities, and special purpose authorities with the power to issue tax-exempt bonds can pass on the advantages of low interest rates to projects in target locations. Recent federal legislative limits on the use of revenue bonds for housing dramatically reduced the number of issues planned in 1981. These restrictions should not limit a city's or state's ability to focus on infill projects serving moderate-income purchasers. These programs can be operated directly by local or state authorities or administered through banks and savings and loans under "loan-to-lenders" or mortgage repurchase arrangements.

The most ambitious infill effort to date was formulated jointly by the cities of Minneapolis and St. Paul. In addition to targeting 95 percent of bond proceeds to new construction, the program involved a unique equity participation effort using funds from foundations and labor union pension funds to make new housing ownership more affordable to moderate-income households. In return for providing part of the required downpayment for qualifying purchasers, the foundations and unions will share proportionately in the property's appreciation.

Early revenue bond programs were typically targeted to moderate- and middle-income home purchasers. Both new and existing housing could qualify regardless of location. Los Angeles has a bond program under way that is not geographically targeted. In contrast, Denver issued bonds for new housing in a 40-block redevelopment area.

Revenue bonds are only one of many possible ways of reducing interest rates for infill projects. Birmingham uses

UDAG funds to provide second mortgages for scattered-site single-family infilling on vacant lots in otherwise built-up subdivisions, as well as for larger projects. Interest rates are subsidized below prevailing FHA rates. Costs have been further reduced on programs that combine local incentives with Section 235 or other federal subsidy programs.

State housing finance agencies have also been involved in infill projects. For example, the New Jersey Mortgage Finance Agency's Neighborhood Loan Program operates in 25 designated locations that have experienced disinvestment. No limits are placed on buyers' income, but a maximum mortgage amount of $45,000 for single-family homes effectively limits this program to purchasers of existing, rather than new, housing. The Connecticut Housing Finance Authority's Urban Area Program has operated under similar constraints. The state of Arizona's most recent issue provides special set-asides for new housing in areas designated as blighted. California is considering targeting to redevelopment areas. To date, however, most state programs have not provided for special targeting or set-asides for infill housing per se.

Involving Local Development Corporations in Demonstration Projects

Some cities have fostered local development corporations that have had some success with infill construction in seemingly marginal neighborhoods. In Chicago, four such neighborhood-based organizations have combined to obtain a UDAG that will assist in acquisition and development of scattered lots to provide over 100 new owner-occupied housing units with the interest rates subsidized under the Section 235 program. The housing will be built in areas with active Neighborhood Housing Services (NHS) rehabilitation programs. Oakland also has a project with NHS sponsorship. In New York's deteriorated South Bronx neighborhood, new homes are now being built, again using the Section 235 program.

Many of these demonstration projects are heavily subsidized, combining use of surplus publicly owned lots with low-cost financing; some involve UDAG grants. Obviously, such extensive subsidies will not be widespread, nor should they be made available for numerous projects in any one high-risk neighborhood. Yet, if they can bolster confidence in marginal locations, future efforts may require less subsidy.

Increasing Attention to Maintenance and Rehabilitation

In many neighborhoods, upgrading of the existing building stock will be needed before developers can be convinced that new housing or commercial uses are a sound investment. If existing structure values are low, builders will be unable to construct new infill housing without subsidies. If vandalism, poor maintenance, and abandonment are evident, infill lots will be unmarketable for most uses regardless of their size, zoning, or other attributes. As a long-term strategy, cities should promote ongoing maintenance and substantial rehabilitation in those neighborhoods or subdivisions appearing to have strong infill potential.

Public Service Improvements

Cities and suburbs need to pay attention to ongoing maintenance and repair needs for roads, bridges, utilities, and public buildings as part of an overall infill strategy. Overburdened service delivery systems and inadequate roads or water pressure can deter infilling, especially at a large scale. Housekeeping services, such as street cleaning and garbage pickup, also merit special attention in areas targeted for infilling. Phoenix is one city that has identified litter, abandoned cars, and other physical problems as major deterrents to infilling because of the poor image projected by careless maintenance. Unfortunately, elected officials in most cities are extremely reluctant to target additional maintenance crews or capital improvement dollars to one or a few neighborhoods while providing lower levels of service elsewhere. Capital budgeting processes should consider how to garner political support for infill target area programs.

Nondevelopment or Interim Uses

In areas where a market for infill lots has yet to appear, cities have adopted various strategies for improving their physical appearance and utility to the neighborhood. Some cities will sell publicly owned vacant parcels to adjacent property owners for a nominal sum. "Lotsteading" is used by a number of cities with a high incidence of scattered, small vacant lots that are tax delinquent. Philadelphia, Wilmington, and New York City are three examples. Small residential lots are typically given to adjacent property owners at little cost (often as low as $1) as long as owners agree to maintain the lot and to pay the taxes. Neighborhood groups have established gardens in Cleveland, Los Angeles, Newark, Philadelphia, and St. Louis. Other sites have been improved for parking or as play lots.

Cities are eager to allow these uses as a means of controlling neighborhood blight, but they are reluctant to undertake new long-term maintenance responsibilities. Where lots are deeded to adjacent property owners or neighborhood groups, the property owners must demonstrate that they have the resources to keep the site clean and to repair playground equipment or paving as needed. It is very expensive for city park crews to supervise scattered tot lots. Despite pressure from local residents, park and recreation agencies are reluctant to accept new permanent maintenance obligations. The city of Wilmington, for example, requires neighborhood groups to sign a contract with the city in which they agree to maintain small parks in return for obtaining federal CDBG funds to make improvements. However, the city retains title to the land.

When considering such nondevelopment alternatives for vacant lots, city officials should recognize that title transfers and expensive site improvements imply that city policy will continue to favor keeping the property vacant. Neighbors using vest-pocket parks, surplus parking, or community gardens will be reluctant to give them up later, if and when private development proposals surface. This is not to say that nondevelopment alternatives should be discouraged. They can be valuable in overall neighborhood upgrading. However, if the city intends them to be temporary (and subject to change at a later date), this must be made clear to adjacent property owners and other interested users. New York City's Green Thumb Program provides these controls by leasing lots to neighborhood permanent improvements, and by allowing termination of the lease if permanent uses are found.

Objectives. To encourage inner-city development without federal participation.

Description. The city provides financial guarantees covering land assembly costs to developers willing to construct homes near downtown. If such houses fail to sell within a specified time period (usually 3–4 years), the city will guarantee repurchase of remaining land at a cost not to exceed $3.25 per square foot. The guarantee is most effective at the initial stage of the project because the repurchase price is fixed, based on the land value at the time of purchase. Land is assembled privately (without the assistance of eminent domain). Under the Areawide Redevelopment Program, the developer also has flexibility to use innovative development standards that are less restrictive (e.g., using a planned development district).

Accomplishments. To date, one developer (Fox and Jacobs) has agreed to participate. The developer is purchasing approximately 80 acres of noncontiguous properties and is constructing Bryan Place. The first phase is a 14-acre site containing approximately 63 single-family detached units. These units are selling for $100,000 to $120,000. Subsequent phases will include single-family attached units to increase densities near the CBD.

Costs. The program was capitalized out of the city's federal revenue-sharing fund. The initial authorization was for $10 million; however, only $2 million has actually been put into the reserve fund. At this point, none of the funds have been spent. The Bryan Place project has been successful, and the city has not had to repurchase any of the land.

Eligible Locations. Any property within a two-mile radius of downtown is eligible. Bryan Place is located approximately ½ mile from downtown. It is a lower-income area with mixed residential and commercial uses. The site is between two major employment centers, the CBD and Baylor University Hospital.

Contact.
E. Jack Schoop
Planning Director
City Hall
Dallas, Texas 75201
(214) 670-4127

Objectives. To encourage infilling and new housing development in general through the use of tax-exempt financing and equity participation, thus providing greater homeownership opportunity for persons with low and moderate incomes. The program is also intended to increase employment in the construction industry.

Description. The Housing and Redevelopment Authorities of the cities of Minneapolis and St. Paul entered into a joint powers agreement to issue tax-exempt revenue bonds to provide low-cost mortgages for purchase of owner-occupied housing. Local bond funds will be combined with a private foundation grant and a UDAG to further reduce housing costs to prospective homeowners through equity participation. The project focuses on new, energy-efficient, common-wall and family-oriented housing, although some of the monies will be used for financing purchase of existing housing. Approximately 9.5 percent of the mortgage proceeds ($199.5 million) available for mortgage financing will be used to finance newly constructed housing units not exceeding $77,880 in cost. The effective interest rate will be roughly 11 percent.

Under the joint powers agreement, the cities created a single agency, the Family Housing Fund, to administer the program. The effect of using equity participation as a method of assisting home purchase is to allow participation of families whose income is lower than that which can be helped using only low-interest mortgages derived from sale of the housing revenue bonds. The Family Housing Fund will contribute up to 25 percent of the equity in a house and will share proportionately in the increase in equity at the time of future sale. The outstanding principal and appreciation share will be paid at the time of sale; the proportional increase in value will be returned to the Family Housing Fund.

Accomplishments. The UDAG application was submitted. Bonds were expected to be sold in mid-June 1981. In the past, both cities have issued other housing revenue bonds. Minneapolis provided approximately 1,800 loans to individuals and families through four bond issues. St. Paul has issued $50 million worth of mortgage revenue bonds, which assisted 910 households. The vast majority of the homeowners assisted under both programs were first-time homebuyers.

The two cities have the authority to issue $250 million in housing revenue bonds. The two phases of the program (six months each) are expected to provide mortgage assistance for 3,600 to 3,700 housing units.

Costs and Funding Sources. The project will be financed with a $10.1 million UDAG, approximately $250 million of tax-exempt revenue bonds, $6 million from the McKnight Foundation, $55 million to $85 million from labor union pension funds, and $70 million to $120 million from private financial institutions. The following is a summary of the use of funds by source.

Lendable mortgage proceeds: $210 million (revenue bonds)
Discount, cost of issuance: $7.5 million (revenue bonds)
Bond reserve fund: $32.5 million (revenue bonds); $3 million (UDAG)
Equity participation: $5 million loan (McKnight Foundation); $1 million grant (McKnight Foundation); $5 million (labor union pension fund); $7 million (UDAG); Total: $18 million
Construction financing: $50–$80 million (labor union pension fund); $70–$120 million (private financial institutions)
Administration: $100,000 (UDAG)

Eligible Locations. Projects in all areas of both Minneapolis and St. Paul are eligible. Over 100 sites in each city have been identified. Up to 20 percent of the mortgage proceeds in the first phase can be set aside for designated redevelopment areas. During the first six months after the bond issue, half of the mortgage proceeds will be used to assist households with incomes of $23,500 or less (median income is currently $23,600). All additional funds (i.e, equity participation and graduated assistance payment grant) are targeted to lower-income households and are tied solely to the first phase of the program.

In the second six-month phase, the maximum income limit will increase to $25,960. Although the maximum house price is $77,880 for both phases, the average cost of new home construction is only $57,000 in Minneapolis and $65,000 in St. Paul.

Contact.
Larry Walker
Director of Mortgage Operations
Minneapolis Community Development Agency
217 S. 3rd Street
Minneapolis, Minnesota 55401
(612) 348-4662

Objectives. To begin the renewal of the Pioneer Park portion of the city by providing low-cost, single-family housing for low-income families.

Description. A 43-block area on the east side of Springfield has been set aside for comprehensive redevelopment. The first phase consists of development of housing on 12 lots in Block 31. Development is financed by a loan secured by The First Federal Bank of Springfield from the Federal Home Loan Bank and will be undertaken by a specially formed local development corporation. The program offers four key incentives for prospective owners to buy and build on the lots: (1) low interest (at 12 percent plus two points); (2) five percent downpayment; (3) city's gift of the lot; (4) the setting aside of CDBG funds for small grants to prospective buyers to cover closing and other ancillary costs. If after five years the buyer has not improved the lot or has failed to occupy it, it reverts to the city.

Accomplishments. Construction of the first units was scheduled to begin during the summer of 1981.

Eligible Locations. Pioneer Park is located on Springfield's east side. It is a predominantly black and Italian neighborhood, which has been the site of most public housing projects and redevelopment efforts.

Costs. The city forgoes the value of the lots, which had been acquired under earlier urban renewal programs. In addition, it has allocated $50,000 in CDBG funds to help with closing costs. Commitments for $1.25 million in private mortgage funds have been secured.

Contact.
Willis Logan, Jr., Director
Community Development Department
601 East Jefferson Street
Springfield, Illinois 62701
(217) 789-2377

Objectives. To assist developers in providing affordable housing units for families.

Description. A twofold housing production program has been launched based on a land writedown program for Section 8 family projects and mortgage revenue bond financing for owner-occupied housing. The land writedown is available to cover the gap between the available HUD mortgage and the developer's equity contribution (approximately 15 percent). Some of the funds have also been used as revolving loans to enable sponsors to maintain site control. Deed restrictions assure that the developments continue to serve lower-income households.

The mortgage revenue bond financing program, which reduces the monthly housing payment for participating buyers by up to $250, has enabled many households in the $20,000–$30,000 income range to qualify for new homes. The program, by providing permanent financing, enables developers to obtain construction financing.

Accomplishments. Seven Section 8 land writedown projects totaling 162 units have been started. Projects representing an additional 149 units have received interim loans, in return for deeds of trust and deed restrictions, in order to prevent loss of site control while awaiting FHA firm commitment.

A total of 577 units have been included in the city's first citywide mortgage subsidy program.

Constraints. The land writedown for Section 8 projects is necessary because the HUD fair market rents do not reflect land costs in Los Angeles, which are among the highest in the country. High land costs also have made it difficult to provide mortgages to as large and diverse a range of projects as the city would have preferred under its mortgage bond program. A difficult bond market, necessitating higher interest rates, has intensified this problem.

Costs. The city council has allotted about $8 million in CDBG funds for land writedown assistance for the Section 8 writedown program, and $1.5 million for a public housing authority revolving fund to allow land purchase for new public housing. Under the mortgage bond program, $45 million in bonds were sold.

Eligible Locations. Any location within the city is eligible. The city has selected some sites for development, but developers are generally expected to find their own sites. Twenty-six different sites were covered in the bond issue. Also, the city will not approve projects oriented to the elderly until a sufficient number of family units has been obtained.

Contact.
Kathleen M. Connell, Director of Housing
City of Los Angeles
215 W. 6th Street, Room 700
Los Angeles, California 90014
(213) 485-3406

These units in Los Angeles were financed by the mortgage revenue bond program.

Objectives. To create stability in neighborhoods by making quality affordable housing available to existing residents.

Description. A total of 104 new Section 235 housing units for owner occupancy are planned. NHS will construct 24 of these units in the Heart of Chicago neighborhood. The remainder will be built in other locations under the sponsorship of four neighborhood groups. UDAG funds will help write down the purchase price of the homes, and the Neighborhood Reinvestment Corporation will contribute up to $3,000 for downpayments on the NHS units. Subsidies bring the cost down to allowable Section 235 sale price limits.

Accomplishments. Phase I of the project is complete; four units were constructed and sold for $44,500 each. A grant from Neighborhood Reinvestment Corporation helped to write down the cost of the mortgages. In Phase II, nearly all of the lots have been acquired. The few remaining lots will be bought from the city's holdings of demolition liens at a reduced price. The units will sell for $52,800.

Constraints. Primary constraints were time related—it took a long time for UDAG approval and selection of a contractor. Other constraints include high interest rates and delays in finding financing for a conventional development in an area that has had no new single-family construction in over 60 years.

Costs. The project involves a $1.83 million UDAG, along with $5.1 million in private funds. First Federal Savings and Loan of Chicago has committed to make takeout mortgages a part of the Section 235 program; Pioneer Bank and Continental Bank will provide interim financing. HUD's Section 235 program will provide mortgage insurance and interest subsidies to help low-income families finance purchase of the units.

Eligible Locations. Phase I units are located in the NHS Heart of Chicago neighborhood. Phase II units sponsored will be in the Heart of Chicago and Near Northwest neighborhoods, which are characterized by older housing and strong family ties. (Heart of Chicago's population is predominantly Latino and ethnic white.) Remaining units will be built in other moderate-income neighborhoods.

Contact.
Andy Ditton
Associate Director for Development Activities
Neighborhood Housing Services
123 North Jefferson Street
Chicago, Illinois 60606
(312) 454-0290

Objectives. To begin the repopulation and strengthening of South Bronx neighborhoods through homeownership. The city has noted that pockets of small, owner-occupied housing have best withstood the general abandonment and disintegration of the area.

Description. HUD Section 235 homeownership subsidy funds are being used to finance 250 units of single-family housing in the South Bronx, where nearly one-third of the land area is currently vacant. The housing will be built on city-owned land in four locations and will be 75 percent three-bedroom and 25 percent four-bedroom. This will be the first time that Section 235 has been used for any large-scale project in the city of New York.

Accomplishments. Despite the devastation of the South Bronx, over 1,000 families have signed up to purchase the 250 proposed units. Model home construction began in May 1981.

Constraints. The proposal initially met with considerable skepticism from participating agencies because of deteriorated conditions in the South Bronx.

Eligible Locations. Four sites have been chosen to take advantage of locations that are almost entirely vacant, yet still are within or near strong neighborhoods.

Costs. Total construction cost is estimated at $15 million. A $3.7-million UDAG to defray project costs has been approved. CDBG funds are being used for some minor demolition, site preparation, and relocation, although most of these sites are vacant.

Contact.
Joe Cicciu
Section 235 Project Manager
South Bronx Development Organization
529 Courtlandt Avenue
New York City, New York 10451
(212) 993-7850

Objectives. To promote development of city-owned surplus lots and to provide new housing units for moderate-income persons.

Description. The Oakland Owner-Built Housing Program provides for the construction of single-family residences on infill lots using sweat equity. The program began in June 1980 and initially received 300 applications. A NHS committee selected program participants. City-owned surplus properties were sold to NHS for $3,000 per lot—only 20 percent of the full market value.

The building process includes subcontracting for electrical, plumbing, sheetrock, stucco, and cement work. However, the owner/builders will provide the required labor to complete construction. Tasks that are the responsibility of the owner/builder include platting, concrete pouring, digging footings, joisting the subfloor, insulating walls, erecting trusses, roof sheeting, installing windows, landscaping, and installing fences. The total amount of the loan for each house is $46,000, and the value of the house on the market is estimated at $80,000. Oakland NHS was designated as the borrower as a protective measure in case the initial owner/builder dropped out of the program.

Eligible Locations. To qualify for the program, prospective participants had to have income of at least $21,000 and not more than $31,000 annually.

Accomplishments. Benefits of the program include:
- construction of 14 single-family homes
- participants' ability to assume home maintenance chores
- significant construction cost savings for participant
- heightened sense of neighborhood pride.

Costs. Total cost of program, including loans, land, interest, and technical assistance, was $625,000 for 14 homes.

Contact.
Wilbert Lee, Director
Paul Dixon, Construction Manager
Oakland Neighborhood Housing Services, Inc.
1641 98th Avenue
Oakland, California 94603
(415) 632-8892

Objectives. To improve the image and aesthetics of poorer neighborhoods throughout the city so as to begin the process of making them desirable areas again and to provide community amenities in the interim.

Description. Operation Green Thumb is a small agency within the city's Department of General Services (DGS also contains the Department of Real Property) created to administer short-term leases for use of vacant municipal land as parks and gardens. The land must be city-owned and have no other use planned for the coming 12 to 14 months. Operation Green Thumb is approached by groups interested in particular parcels. It determines whether the land is held by the city and whether other uses are contemplated. If the land is found to be available, it is leased to the group for $1 per year. Only bona fide nonprofit community organizations are eligible. Leases forbid permanent development and are subject to revocation with 30-day notice if a permanent use potential emerges. Green Thumb also works with some groups to aid lot improvements, providing design services, a limited amount of soil, plants, lumber, and fencing.

Accomplishments. The program has received vocal neighborhood support and enhanced the attractiveness of previously vacant lots. Approximately 700 lots are leased at present under the program (some sites have multiple lots). The operation expects soon to have 120 fully developed parks, gardens, and play lots. Prior to the establishment of Green Thumb, the process for determining ownership of vacant lots was cumbersome and imprecise, and the city had no mechanism for dealing with interim use requests.

Constraints. The Green Thumb operation has proven difficult to administer from a management standpoint due to absence of provisions for such activity in existing municipal practice. It has experienced extensive management turnover since its creation in 1978 and is only now settling into a workable routine.

Costs. Total budget is roughly $350,000 annually, which includes a full-time staff of four. Five other staff persons are on loan to the agency from other departments.

Contact.
Ken Davies, Director
Operation Green Thumb
NYC Department of General Services
49 Chambers Street, Room 1020
New York City, New York 10007
(212) 233-2926

Objectives. Interim uses of vacant lots are intended to make neighborhoods more attractive to developers and residents, as well as to provide community amenities.

Description. The city of Wilmington has worked with local community groups to develop interim uses for vacant sites that will benefit the community. The parcels are temporarily improved as gardens, parks, parking, and play areas. Community groups or individuals must agree in writing to maintain the lots. Responsibilities include tree trimming, grass cutting, weed removal, and snow removal.

Accomplishments. Several lots have been redeveloped to varying degrees. The city published a catalog describing the program and setting forth the costs of various improvements.

Constraints. This is an informal program with no staff of its own, and the amount of effort that could be devoted to such activity has fluctuated with the availability and interest of housing and planning staff. Moreover, the city has been concerned with not overextending its obligations, as properties that the community groups fail to keep up become a maintenance responsibility of the city's.

Costs. The program thus far has not had formal status and has required only intermittent allocations of staff time. CDBG funds are used to defray costs for benches, play equipment, and lighting.

Contact.
Bessie Evans
Department of Real Estate and Housing
City of Wilmington
800 North French Street
Wilmington, Delaware 19801
(302) 571-4057

Addressing Site-Specific Problems

A number of limiting physical or environmental conditions can affect the developability of sites that, by virtue of regional market conditions and location, would otherwise be good candidates for infilling. Other problems can be posed by excessively high land costs that are common for infill sites.

In most markets, infill land is expensive vis-a-vis buying and improving raw acreage at the urban fringe. Ways must be found to reduce per unit infill land costs; otherwise, infill projects will be largely limited to luxury housing and fast-food restaurants or other retail uses generating high per-square-foot sales. There are various ways in which cities can reduce the effective cost of land, both directly and indirectly.

Land Writedown

Cities have been using land writedowns since the early years of federal urban renewal programs in the 1950s. The city acquires the land and then resells it to a developer at a reduced price. Municipal funds can be used to make up the difference, as can federal CDBG, UDAG, or EDA funds, depending on the nature and location of the proposed development. A number of programs described in this chapter combine land writedowns with other incentives to produce low- and moderate-income housing, especially in high-cost locations (such as New York and Los Angeles) where high land prices make it difficult to build within cost limits set by federal programs.

Land Leasing

Cities can also lease land they already own (or acquire) to a developer at attractive rates. A long-term ground lease can be very attractive because it reduces a developer's equity requirements and can increase the leverage in a project. Also, rent payments are deductible for federal income tax purposes as a business expense. Because land is not a depreciable asset, leasing can be a very powerful development incentive for those cities that already own attractive vacant parcels or have the resources to acquire them. The city of San Diego operates an extensive leasing program that has been used to encourage construction of low- and moderate-income housing using Section 8 subsidies. Smaller California cities have also used leasing, as has Portland, Oregon (but on a much smaller scale than San Diego).

Because of the potentially high public cost involved in land acquisition (either for sale or lease), the use of land writedowns or leasing should be limited to projects offering unique opportunities (for achieving scale economies or mixed uses) or meeting special public objectives (providing market rate housing near CBDs, scattered site assisted housing, or new jobs). Because of the need to minimize front end costs, cities to date have largely limited their leasing programs to sites they already own or control. In most cases, land acquisition should not proceed without a committed developer who presents a detailed plan for the site. This will avoid having the city buy land and then finding itself unable to dispose of it promptly.

Obviously, there can be exceptions to this rule—i.e., a one-time-only chance to obtain land at a reduced price from other government bodies or private estates.

Tax Incentives

Property tax abatement is yet another way of reducing the high cost of infill development. It will be most attractive in locations that are at a significant competitive disadvantage vis-a-vis outlying jurisdictions with respect to overall tax burdens. New York City, St. Louis, and Kansas City are all examples of cities extensively using tax abatement for various commercial and residential projects; even more jurisdictions offer these incentives to industry. In most states, however, enabling legislation does not allow targeting tax abatements only to infill projects or to redevelopment in areas with lagging investment activity.

The importance of tax reductions as an incentive will vary from project to project. In some cases, it will be critical in influencing a reluctant developer to try an infill project; but in others, it will have no impact on his/her decision. Cities must carefully evaluate the financial projections of projects for which tax reductions are requested to assure that such "carrots" are needed to stimulate development activity.

In a few isolated cases, the feasibility of infill projects is threatened by past property tax delinquencies that must be paid before a parcel can be sold. To the extent that these outstanding obligations significantly raise land acquisition costs, they can deter otherwise worthwhile projects. Cities and counties should consider waiving the back taxes on these sites if given a written commitment that development will proceed within a maximum of, say, 18 months. (If development did not occur, the owner would be responsible for the back taxes.)

Unfortunately, not all states permit municipalities to exercise this discretion. Only a handful of states provide for automatic transfer of tax delinquent properties to local governments after expiration of the redemption period. In addition, redemption periods can be lengthy. Certain states have established procedures to reduce delays (New York, New Jersey, Maryland, Massachusetts). Designed primarily to recycle vacant, tax delinquent structures, these statutes can also apply to vacant lots.

One example of a workable program is in Polk County, Iowa (Des Moines), where back taxes are waived on lots delinquent for three years or more if a developer agrees to build new housing meeting city codes on a specified time schedule. Duluth, Minnesota, has a similar program.

Density Bonuses/Variances

Allowing developers to make more intense use of their sites is another indirect method of reducing land costs. Incentives could include density bonuses or variances from side yard, setback, or parking requirements. The use of density bonuses is common in cities that have special zoning provisions for their central business districts. To date, bonus systems have had their greatest effect in stimulating CBD office construction. However, cities are now beginning to target bonuses to CBD housing, as witnessed by new programs in Phoenix and Portland.

Cities can also offer bonuses for projects outside the CBD that provide public amenities and outstanding design solutions for small or oddly shaped lots. Again, proposals will have to be reviewed on a case-by-case basis, which could increase the work load for city staffs in an era of budget cutting.

Fee Waivers

Utility hookup fees, subdivision filing fees, and building permits do not constitute a very high proportion of total construction costs in most cities and suburbs. However, cities such as Omaha and Phoenix that waive these fees for infill projects find that a special effort to reduce costs—even for small items—generates good will

among builders and can cause them to consider locations they previously would have ignored. The amount of city revenue foregone is minimal. Developments must still meet all technical requirements for permit issuance.

Correcting Infrastructure Problems

Many infill sites require minor extensions of existing utility lines, replacement or repair activities, or road access improvements. In addition, partially served parcels are common in many suburban areas where control over utility service is fragmented. The existing low-density residences and businesses may front on arterial streets but are still served by septic systems. Larger urban sites may have problems requiring relocation of utility easements or railroad trackage or removal of buried materials. These problems can be particularly acute when assembling vacant and underutilized parcels for industrial redevelopment. It makes sense to give priority to the improvement of these sites.

Where infrastructure problems are localized and markets are strong, developers will bear the cost of correcting them, and they will not be deterrents to infilling. However, these corrections are costly, which could make the price of infill residential, commerical, or industrial space noncompetitive in weaker markets.

Engineering department staff should identify whether there are physical constraints or basic infrastructure problems with promising sites. If there are problems, it is important to determine whether the expected use (or proposed use if a developer is at hand) will provide sufficient benefits to justify public expenditure to solve the problem. In some cases, improvements may be made in advance of development (particularly in a strong market); but in others, a specific development proposal should be required before an improvement is made.

A special capital fund for small-scale projects would be useful in meeting the timing requirements of prospective developers. Providing upgraded infrastructure as part of ongoing capital improvement programming is an accepted government activity, but money for capital projects is all too scarce. Difficulties arise when proposed improvements are perceived to benefit new construction, while existing homeowners and businesses must continue to cope with potholes, drainage problems, or inadequate water pressure. To gain public support, major infrastructure maintenance and upgrading should be targeted to benefit both new and existing buildings so that existing property owners feel they would reap some benefits as well.

Private Financing Techniques: Tax Increment Financing (TIF) and Special Improvement Districts

Improvements in public facilities serving larger infill projects can be financed using tax increment bonds. Future increases in tax revenues generated by new development are targeted specifically for retiring bonds used to fund public improvements. (Land writedown costs could also be part of a tax increment program.) Enabling legislation for this innovative financing program has been passed in a number of states. Project experience is extensive in California, Minnesota, and Iowa. The use of tax increment financing (TIF) has largely been limited to commercial or mixed-use projects, especially those in or near central business districts. Not all states allow TIF, and limits on permitted tax increases (such as were stimulated by the success of California's Proposition 13) could jeopardize the viability of TIF programs.

Road, utility, and drainage improvements can increase the development potential of vacant lots and enhance the value of existing buildings. If a need for action is perceived, property owners may want to form a special district to tax themselves for the cost of improvements. Where permitted by state law, these districts can issue tax-exempt bonds that provide advantages over conventional financing normally available to private developers (i.e., longer repayment terms, lower interest rates). Such districts have long been used to finance utility extensions in the suburbs of Houston, Omaha, and Seattle. The same technique can be used for infill areas. If owners of existing buildings are asked to participate, they will want to be sure that bona fide development plans exist for vacant sites within the district so that improved sites will not bear a disproportionate share of the increased tax burden.

Flexibility in Meeting Infrastructure Requirements

Not all developers will require or desire public financial assistance with infrastructure improvements. Many are willing to bear the costs themselves but are looking for creativity and flexibility from city engineering staff who review their plans. Special procedures should be established to identify potential problems quickly and resolve them without submitting small infill projects to the same standards required of traditional suburban subdivisions.

Objectives. To create additional standard housing in an inner city neighborhood.

Description. Land cleared for the I-505 right-of-way became state surplus when this proposed highway was dropped from the interstate system. The city of Portland bought three sites that it felt could be redeveloped in harmony with neighborhood plans. The land is being leased for a 60-year term.

Accomplishments. One of the sites was used for a townhouse project. A subsidized lease ($2,500/year) was necessary to enable the developer to use Section 8 for all units. The 30-unit townhouse project is complete and fully occupied. A parcel located two blocks away is now being considered for middle-income owners.

Constraints. The development commission reports that the only problem was getting a street vacation for parking. The vacation was necessary because the Portland code requires one parking space for every housing unit constructed. Angle parking was implemented on the vacated street. The commission worked closely with neighborhood residents before plans were put in final form.

Eligible Area. All three pieces bought by the PDC were in the Thurman/Vaughn Corridor, a close-in neighborhood also containing industrial land uses.

Costs. This project was part of a package recommended in a comprehensive corridor development study. The study portion, which included the Upshur House condominium and other improvements within one block, cost approximately $100,000, plus an estimated $15,000–$20,000 in staff time. The Upshur House parcel cost $182,400. This land was purchased some three years ago.

Contact.
Elaine Howard
Portland Development Commission
1500 S.W. First Avenue
Portland, Oregon 97201
(503) 248-4938

Objectives. To encourage the development of unused public land, thus providing affordable housing opportunities for residents of low and moderate income. It is hoped that the program will ultimately use 200 acres and incorporate open space, a variety of housing types, and a broad income mix.

Description. The city of San Diego has among its landholdings roughly 4,000 acres, much of which is potentially developable for housing. Under this program, city-owned land is leased for 50–55 years to private developers of low- and moderate-income housing units. Two major sites together will have over 800 units, of which 30 percent will be Section 8. In addition, the city council has authorized lease of some land at below-market rates as a further incentive. Reduced rates are based on financial feasibility of the project; normally the annual land lease rate would be 10 percent to 15 percent of the land value. The normal lease rate would have required almost one-third of the project's first year income. The actual lease is roughly six percent of the project's gross revenues, enhancing the project's financial feasibility. The two large projects are to have a mixture of low- and moderate-income units with market rate condominiums. The sale of land under the condominiums has been proposed. Smaller, scattered-site projects are also under development.

Accomplishments. Two projects in the downtown area with 100 percent Section 8 elderly total 350 units on leased land and 100 units on land that was sold. Four other projects are Orchard I (375 units of elderly); Stonewood (253 units, including some families); Orchard II (288 units under construction); and Villa Merced (100 units of Section 202 elderly). All four of these are reduced-rate leases.

Constraints. Some public hostility has been expressed toward low-income housing, as well as opposition to sale of land under condominiums; continuation of the land under the city's control was felt to be preferable. One project was also slowed down by insistence that a park be incorporated into the site and because of a required Coastal Zone Management review process. Many residents believed that long vacant city-owned land should be permanent open space, which creates controversy when housing projects are proposed for the sites.

Costs. Not available.

Contact.
Ben Montijo, Executive Director
San Diego Housing Commission
121 Broadway, Suite 443
San Diego, California 92101
(714) 236-5456

Objectives. Construction of housing units that will be sold to individual buyers at below market rates because no land costs are involved. The program also helps the city and county to achieve a stabilized tax base and aids in the revitalization of declining neighborhoods.

Description. Private developers and the city of Des Moines may request that certain parcels be removed from the county land bank. Back taxes are waived, and the county will subrogate its interest in the lots if developers agree to build housing units in accordance with the city's density provisions and on a specified time schedule. The program began in November 1979. The city of Des Moines revised its zoning ordinance at the same time to permit single-family homes on smaller lots and fee simple townhouse ownership. Three-year tax abatements are also available for homes in designated revitalization areas.

Costs and Funding. CDBG monies are used to provide utilities for the sites at a cost of up to $2,000 per lot. Iowa Housing Finance Agency and HUD Section 235 financing were used to further reduce costs in certain projects.

Eligible Locations. All areas of the city are eligible to participate in the program as long as there are available county-owned parcels. In order to be eligible, the homebuyer's income must not exceed $17,300 (adjusted gross income). In addition, 50 percent or more of the housing units built must meet low- to moderate-income guidelines set by FHA/VA or the Iowa Housing Finance Authority. Further, 50 percent or more of all housing units must be $55,000 or lower in price. Developers are permitted to sell a "land bank house" whose costs exceed $55,000 if the preceding conditions are met. Although some land bank parcels are located in suburban Polk County, the housing program operates only in Des Moines.

Accomplishments.
- Program is responsible for the construction of over $5 million of housing in 1980. This represents the single most substantial source of housing activity in the Des Moines area. The program is largely responsible for the construction activity of many of the small developers/homebuilders in Des Moines.
- The program provided reasonably priced housing for low- and moderate-income families in the Des Moines metropolitan area. The houses, averaging 1,100 square feet, range from $30,000 to $48,000 fully equipped and are of quality construction.
- The program enabled quality housing to be constructed in built-up areas without disrupting the neighborhoods.
- One hundred and twenty homes were built as a result of the first two phases of the land bank program. Another 108 lots have been placed in the program for phases three and four.

Contact.
Gary Pryor, Director
Polk County Physical Planning Department
5895 N.E. 14th Street
Des Moines, Iowa 50313

Objectives. To reduce land costs, thereby facilitating production of 200 to 300 housing units annually.

Description. In 1978, San Mateo County hired a consultant to identify every vacant parcel that could conceivably be developed for family or elderly housing. A number of parcels were then purchased from private owners or other public jurisdictions. The land can be sold at a reduced rate if the developer can show that a writedown is needed to make the project economically feasible. Further, HUD subsidy funds can be used if the rents charged are within the paying ability of low- and moderate-income families. California State Housing Finance Agency funds can also be tapped.

Accomplishments. The county identified 80 sites that were appropriate for housing development. It has purchased, or is negotiating to buy, nine of those sites which vary in cost from $90,000 to $1 million. Development is complete at two of the sites, providing 171 units of Section 8 housing for the elderly. The buildings are fully occupied and have waiting lists.

Constraints. Before a public entity can develop or finance housing for persons of low and moderate income, a local referendum must be approved. This type of referendum is often turned down. The county has also found that negotiating a land purchase from a private owner can sometimes be extremely time consuming.

Costs and Funding Sources. Each year the county sets aside $1 million of its block grant funds for land acquisition.

Eligible Locations. Any locality in the county is eligible to participate once a joint powers agreement has been signed. The county directs its efforts to areas where the land is available and where residents and elected officials indicate political support for the development. Of the completed developments, one is in the unincorporated area of East Palo Alto, which is predominantly black. The other is in Menlo Park, a very well-to-do city.

Contact.
Maurice Dawson,
Program Administrator
Housing and Community Development Division
County Government Center
Redwood City, California 94063
(415) 363-4451

Objectives. To encourage and to facilitate the construction of additional housing by selling publicly owned lands at minimal cost.

Description. The Duluth Housing and Redevelopment Authority acquires and disposes of certain tax-forfeited or city-owned vacant lands by publicizing their availability and selling them. Any person or entity having the financial ability to obtain adequate financing to complete the purchase of a parcel and complete the construction of an approved dwelling is eligible. Construction must begin within six months after purchase of the land and be completed within one year of its commencement date. If these requirements are not met, the land reverts back to the Housing Authority or to the interest of any lender making a mortgage. Applicants are allowed to purchase up to four parcels per year.

Accomplishments. The program has been in operation for 2½ years; 40–50 single-family homes have been constructed on scattered lots processed through the program.

Costs. The city's general fund was used by the housing authority to pay back taxes to St. Louis County for the purchase of any tax-delinquent vacant lots. The lots are being marketed at a price that is sufficient to cover title clearance and minimal administrative costs. Thus, the city's general fund absorbs the difference.

Eligible Locations. The program operates citywide and is not targeted to any geographic area or income group.

Contact.
Ken Johnson
City of Duluth
Office of Business Development
400 City Hall
Duluth, Minnesota 55802
(218) 723-3556

Objectives. To encourage development in two target areas.

Description. The city of Phoenix has waived all planning and building fees in two areas of the city. These fees include platting, variance, use permits, building permits, mechanical systems inspections, and the like. Water and sewer hookup fees are waived except in instances where the service charges are encumbered by bond issue obligations.

Accomplishments. In the year that fee waivers have been in effect, some 60–80 housing units have been started on vacant or underutilized parcels in these two areas. Through a combination of applicable waivers, a builder can save $200 to $3,000 per dwelling unit. (A ceiling has been imposed on waivers available to major commercial developments.)

Constraints. The major check on this program has been caution on the part of the city administration lest it suffer excessive losses in revenue or offer greater incentives than could prudently be justified.

Costs. City planners estimate the first year loss through foregone revenue to be approximately $20,000.

Eligible Areas. Two areas have been designated for waivers—the central area surrounding the core of the city (known as the infill incentive area) and a small portion of south Phoenix, where development stimulation was considered necessary.

Contact.
Richard F. Counts, Planning Director
251 W. Washington
Phoenix, Arizona 85003
(602) 262-6364

Objectives. To encourage more central city plats.

Description. Omaha waived the subdivision fee for central city lots and tripled the fee for suburban lots in 1980. This translates into a roughly $50 reduction of front-end development costs per lot on a typical 10-lot infill subdivision. At the same time, the city's sewer connection fee was raised from $290 to $510 for suburban single-family construction and totally eliminated in the central city.

Accomplishments. The waivers were implemented in 1979. There has been more construction in areas eligible for fee waivers in the interim and a slowdown in suburban areas. City planners feel that fee waivers were a supportive incentive rather than the prime cause of such a change.

It should be noted that the fee waivers form a large percentage reduction in the cost of smaller, less expensive homes and are therefore a greater incentive for infill in moderate-income neighborhoods.

Constraints. There was some opposition on the part of the homebuilders, especially those who owned lots in the areas where fees went up. Staff members explained that fee proceeds were being set aside for new interceptor sewers in those areas.

Eligible Areas. In-city zones A, B, and C indicate the portions of the city of Omaha eligible for the platting fee waiver program; sewer waivers apply to all three in-city zones, plus areas recently annexed by the city.

Costs. The platting fee change required minimal staff time. Restructuring of sewer hookup charges necessitated the development of a $50,000 sewer study/master plan and an additional $25,000 of city staff time for supervising the study, drafting ordinances, and meeting with area homebuilders and developers. The entire project was funded locally.

Contact.
Jim Ecker
City Planning Department
1819 Farnam Street
Omaha, Nebraska 68183
(402) 444-5214

Objectives. To create a residential environment within the city for people who would otherwise move to the suburbs.

Description. Development of Coldspring (a 375-acre, 3,780-unit new town-in-town) through a variety of innovative tools, including traditional urban renewal financing of land acquisition, infrastructure, roads, and utilities; and revenue bond financing to create a mortgage pool able to make loans at interest rates considerably below prevailing market rates. Innovative design was used to enhance the project's attractiveness.

Accomplishments. To date, 124 townhouses have been completed. An additional 128 units are almost completed. Foundations have been prepared for another 238 units, of which 150 are for the elderly. All units have been sold as condominiums. Plans also call for commercial space.

Constraints. Environmental review at the level of detail currently required would have delayed the project. The project was started in 1969 when review was less detailed. Also, revenue bonds for mortgages are no longer permitted by federal law except for low- and moderate-income housing. Further phases will have higher mortgage rates.

Costs. About $30 million in government costs so far, all of which have been federally funded (urban renewal, CDBG, EDA grants, and a UDAG). Federal funds covered land acquisition and site improvements. Baltimore General Fund money was used to provide construction financing to the developer for the first stage; construction financing for the second stage was obtained privately.

Eligible Locations. The tools cited have been used in blighted areas throughout Baltimore. The Coldspring site is four miles from the city's center. It had been bypassed by previous developers because of unusual terrain conditions and diverse ownership and because site preparation costs were too high.

Contact.
Lawrence H. Merrill
City of Baltimore
Department of Housing &
Community Development
222 E. Saratoga
Baltimore, Maryland 21203
(301) 396-3236

A combination of factors—unusual terrain, diverse ownership, and high site preparation costs—caused the Coldspring site to be bypassed for earlier development.

Townhouse units at Coldspring, four miles from the center of Baltimore.

Objectives. To dispose of excess city-owned land, the city has decided to actively encourage new low-density for-sale housing that will promote home ownership for city residents who have been shut out of the housing market.

Description. New York City is providing surplus, publicly owned land for housing development in the largest construction program ever undertaken under the Section 235 program. The city advertises parcels for development proposals, selects proposals, and then sells lots for $500 apiece. Developers are responsible for obtaining their own construction financing. Most of the houses will be one-family units in attached rows, two or three stories high. In addition to the Section 235 mortgage interest reduction, homebuyers are eligible to receive either a 10-year or 20-year tax abatement on the improvements. Some builders will use the Section 235 housing as a fallback to test the market, while building larger units with more amenities for buyers with conventional financing. The mix of publicly assisted versus private-market units will be determined by demand.

Accomplishments. Thirteen builders have been selected to construct nearly 2,300 housing units. The city is currently in the process of finalizing arrangements to sell the land and expects that all units will be constructed within two to three years.

Constraints. Due to a cumbersome city approval process, six to nine months are needed to sell the land and transfer title. Because of the lengthy review process, builders have expressed concern that increases in construction costs and the interest rate could result in prices that would be beyond the means of the market for which the houses were originally intended. Also, Section 235 sales price limits ($57,000 for a three-bedroom; $66,000 for a four-bedroom) are too low to produce and to sell a single-family house. The city makes up the difference using UDAG and city funds.

Costs. The city has committed about $10,000 per unit, which will come from the city's capital budget and CDBG. In addition, $3.2 million in UDAG funds are available for two sites in South Bronx and Brooklyn where three builders will get $14,300 per unit toward the construction cost of a total of 226 units.

Eligible Locations. Twenty-four sites have been chosen in urban renewal and community development areas where city-owned land has long been available but where there is no chance of new construction without a subsidy that could bring down the cost to the buyer. Areas where sites have been identified are: Flatbush, Brownsville, East New York, Coney Island, Bedford-Stuyvesant, Bushwick, Bronx and South Bronx, Queens, Manhattan, and Staten Island.

City residents earning from about $21,750 to $38,900 may be eligible for federal mortgage assistance. There are no income limits for persons purchasing the units without mortgage subsidies.

Contact.
Timothy Flanagan, Coordinator
Homeownership Development Program
100 Gold Street
New York, New York 10038
(212) 566-0025

Increasing Land Availability

A major obstacle to infill development is posed by fragmented ownership of larger vacant tracts, especially in central cities. The reluctance of many owners to develop their sites or to sell/lease them for development by others has also been documented. Local governments can do little to force development, but they can help private developers overcome obstacles to large-scale development. In some cases, the city will have to act as an intermediary, assembling the parcels for resale to the private sector.

During the 1950s and 1960s, many cities established urban renewal programs for this purpose. However, weak market conditions left cities holding large tracts of land for many years; plans were often announced but did not materialize. These disappointing results, combined with the merging of the federal renewal program into community development block grants, caused cities to be reluctant to engage in land assembly activities in the 1970s. The high cost of acquisition and relocation, along with the political controversies inherent in demolition programs, resulted in little public involvement in creating large-scale development opportunities.

However, with renewed interest in urban revitalization and close-in living in recent years, the better located large tracts have received greater attention from developers. Recent projects have involved not only vacant land but also underutilized sites, such as rail yards, institutional property, former country clubs, and the like.

In the future, cities may once more have to take an active role in assisting with land assembly. This will be especially true if current program concepts for inner city enterprise zones are implemented. This is not to say that the mistakes of the urban renewal program should be repeated. A committed developer with an approved plan and demonstrated financial backing should be a prerequisite to city action. And small multi-parcel projects (in the 2- to 10-acre range) in city neighborhoods or suburban areas should receive public attention, as well as the 40-acre, large-scale projects close to downtowns. Flexibility will be needed in determining the types and locations of projects to be assisted. Funds available to cities under the CDBG and UDAG programs offer this flexibility, which was lacking under earlier federal urban renewal programs.

Using Eminent Domain

For projects offering unique opportunities to meet community development objectives, a city may be able to use its eminent domain power to acquire land for resale to an interested developer. Such powers should be limited to special situations in which a developer is committed to a definite project. In many states, exercising eminent domain power is a lengthy and difficult process. It can be hard to prove that a legitimate public purpose is served if the land is to be used for a strictly private project. Legal fees are high, and proceedings can take as long as five years.

In Missouri, cities are permitted to transfer limited eminent domain powers directly to private developers who propose construction programs consistent with public objectives. Once the project is approved, the city does not have to be involved in legal proceedings for acquiring individual sites. St. Louis and Kansas City have made extensive use of this technique, mainly for redevelopment efforts.

Land Swapping

City officials should be willing to trade publicly owned properties with private investors when mutual benefits are apparent. By giving up a piece of surplus public land, the city can gain title to another site that might be better suited for public facilities, such as parks, fire stations, or libraries. In turn, developers obtain a site that can be a key component in a large project or has location advantages not needed by the city for its own purposes. The city can also facilitate land trades between two private property owners. Trades are financially attractive to private property owners because they can avoid the capital gains taxes associated with outright sale; they should be encouraged where permitted.

Taxing Vacant Land at Higher Rates

Another approach to encouraging owners to develop vacant land is to tax land at its full market value. This is a dramatic departure from our current system. Data collected for the 1977 Census of Governments confirm that assessment/sales ratios are typically far lower—and less uniform—for vacant land than for single-family homes or other types of improved real estate. Officially, most states mandate that land and improvements must be taxed at the same rates.

Some tax reform advocates recommend a shift to a site-value-based property tax, which would result in vacant properties paying the same taxes as nearby improved sites. No assessment jurisdictions in the United States have adopted this approach, although it is used extensively in Australia and New Zealand. A few cities, such as Pittsburgh and Harrisburg, Pennsylvania, have applied higher tax rates to vacant lots. These special rates are applicable only to municipal taxes—not those levied by schools or other special districts. The differential rates are established primarily to raise additional revenues and not to promote infilling. Officials in these cities have no clear sense of whether heavier land taxation has encouraged infill.

Differential taxation has probably spurred some new development, but it may also have led to greater tax delinquency for other parcels. This indicates a critical problem with tax-related solutions to land vacancy problems. It is impossible to adapt assessment practices to apply only in areas where development should be encouraged and a market is likely to emerge if given a proper push. There can be unintended side effects of higher land taxes. Buildings in areas that are under market pressures to redevelop at higher densities will also feel the effect of higher land taxes, leading to owner pressure for more intense zoning designations than are appropriate. The impact would also be felt by owners who would like to sell their vacant land but are located in areas where property is unmarketable; this could cause increased tax delinquencies if assessors are not sensitive to very localized market conditions.

Land Banking

Land banking programs in most jurisdictions are limited to advance acquisition of sites for future public works projects or municipal facilities. Other properties have been obtained as gifts or through tax delinquency proceedings. Few governments have the resources to actively acquire sites for housing or economic development. Consequently, assemblage of large tracts is a very slow process. In addition, these properties are often concentrated in the more deteriorated neighborhoods where it will be difficult to find developers willing to build housing without subsidies or lenders willing to back projects without at least a partial loan guarantee.

State legislation can limit the ability of counties and cities to obtain title to tax delinquent sites or to accept land donations. The possibility of changing state tax delinquency provisions should be explored; Cleveland's land banking program was established only after a lengthy lobbying effort in the Ohio legislature.

A number of states have authorized establishment of land reutilization authorities (LRAs). These bodies can acquire land through foreclosure or donation, purchase sites needed to aggregate larger tracts, and dispose of land to developers or community groups. A listing of cities with LRAs is provided in Figure 3-3. Detailed information is provided on the St. Louis and Omaha agencies. It should be noted that the success of LRAs in stimulating infilling has largely been confined to industrial projects. This is also true for municipal land banks in Baltimore, Milwaukee, and Philadelphia.

At least a few jurisdictions engage in small-scale advance acquisition efforts to assure availability of sites for subsidized housing. County governments and housing authorities are especially likely to find this activity attractive. CDBG funds can be used to cover costs.

Combining Infill Incentives In Effective Strategies

Cities can offer a variety of different tools and incentives for stimulating investment in infill land. With this variety, they can tailor "packages" of incentives to the specific requirements of individual projects. In addition, citywide strategies, such as improved review procedures and code changes, set a tone that tells developers "we want new investment in our city." For many locations with basically strong regional markets, investment can be stimulated merely by changing attitudes.

Many of the programs included in this chapter were formulated locally but relied, at least in part, on federal funding dating as far back as the urban renewal program. More recently, CDBG monies have been used to acquire sites for low- and moderate-income housing and provide infrastructure improvements. UDAG dollars funded second mortgages or reduced interest rates on permanent loans. FHA programs and Section 8 rent subsidies assisted in the use of surplus publicly owned lands and scattered lots remaining in subdivisions. For nonresidential projects, EDA dollars have been used in a similar manner. None of these programs is designed specifically to encourage or to stimulate infilling, but each is applicable for this purpose, as well as for rehabilitation and clearance. Federal agencies can also free up surplus properties that are no longer needed within cities.

Only a few states have been involved in actively assisting infill projects. California, Connecticut, Oregon, Massachusetts, and other states have advocated infilling in their policy plans; however, direct state involvement in local action programs has been limited. There are indications that states will become more active in the future through targeted financing programs, easing of environmental quality regulations, and changes in any state enabling legislation that presently limits municipal land acquisition and disposition powers. Organizing and funding demonstration projects are other appropriate state roles. States should also examine their own surplus land holdings within urban areas and make them available for private reuse.

Figure 3-3
Summary of Land Reutilization Authority (LRA) Programs
in Various American Cities

City	Name of Program	Year Established	Administering Local Agency
Cleveland, Ohio	Land Reutilization Program	1976	Cleveland Department of Community Development
Kansas City, Missouri	Land Trust	1947; restructured in 1969	Land Trust of Jackson County, Missouri. Can operate throughout the county but focuses on Kansas City.
Omaha, Nebraska	Land Reutilization	1974	Omaha Department of City Planning/County Attorney's Office
Philadelphia, Pennsylvania	Gift Property Program	1975	Vacant Property Review Committee (VPRC)
St. Louis, Missouri	Land Reutilization	1971	Land Revitalization Authority

Source: Robert W. Burchell and David Listokin. *The Adaptive Re-Use Handbook*. Rutgers University Center for Urban Policy Research, New Brunswick, New Jersey, 1981. pp. 266–267.

Basic Program Activities	Accomplishments
Acquisition from the Cuyahoga County Prosecutor's Office of in rem tax-fore-closed properties to be sold or leased to private redevelopers or buyers; land banking for possible future usage by various city agencies.	Acquisition of approximately 3,500 delinquent parcels; land banking and sales programs have yet to be implemented. Law permits sale at fair market value without competitive bidding.
Acquisition from the Jackson County Court of in rem tax-foreclosed properties, hold parcels in trust until private buyers are found; sales to private buyers; maintenance of vacant, city-owned lots.	Acquisition of over 4,200 tax-foreclosed properties since 1949; sale of almost 1,000 county-held properties.
Basically similar to those of Kansas City; acquisition and resale of County-held properties taken through tax foreclosure.	Program was not formally implemented until late 1978; as of the end of May 1979, six properties sold at an average price of $5,500.
VPRC accepts title to: 1. tax delinquent or vacant parcels offered as gifts by their owners in return for the waiving of all outstanding municipal liens; 2. properties foreclosed by HUD; and 3. properties foreclosed by the city through in rem tax foreclosure. Disposes of these properties through five alternative methods: 1. land banking; 2. transferral to municipal agencies or nonprofit housing rehabilitation organizations; 3. transferral to private takers; 4. acceptance for city use; and 5. transferral or use of commercial/industrial properties. Possible eminent domain powers to be granted to VPRC in the near future.	As of the end of May 1979 VPRC had disposed of 1,000 properties.
Sale of in rem tax-foreclosed properties to private buyers; land banking; urban homesteading, sale of properties to public and private developers of residential and nonresidential use; similar to Kansas City Land Trust.	Acquisition of over 10,000 in rem properties; sale of approximately 3,000 of them; industrial park development; disposition of land for industrial park development and homesteading; influence on rezoning for commercial and industrial development.

Objectives. To compel property tax payment where possible and to centralize control of tax-delinquent properties until they can be packaged and sold.

Description. The LRA was established by Missouri statute as a mechanism for restoring abandoned urban lots throughout the city to the tax rolls. Tax-delinquent properties not "redeemed" by their owners are sold at a sheriff's sale, where the minimum bid is back taxes plus administrative costs. Land not sold goes to the LRA, which landbanks the property and attempts to market it. LRA sells a list of its buildings to the public for a nominal cost; complete lists of all holdings, including vacant and commercial properties, are available at reproduction cost.

Accomplishments. The program acts as the "muscle in the arm" that makes people pay their taxes: roughly 50 percent of the property against which judgments are issued is disposed of through redemption. Another 20 percent is usually sold at a sheriff's sale. The remaining 30 percent, which cannot be sold, is deeded to the LRA, which maintains it and attempts to market it. LRA sells approximately 1,000 parcels a year. Most of these sales, however, go to adjacent property owners for side yards. A modest amount of new housing construction on these parcels continues despite the extreme softness of the city's current housing market and the location of these sites in deteriorated sections.

Constraints. The largest problem facing the LRA is the cumulative effect of continuing to take possession of the unsold lots: It now holds roughly 6,000 parcels for which there is no immediate market. These properties represent an ever-increasing maintenance burden. Moreover, many of them have structures still standing. The growing number of derelict properties known to belong to the LRA makes it subject to criticism from neighborhood groups.

Infill housing in historic districts presents difficult design problems, and the new structures have been controversial.

Costs. Maintenance of all properties currently costs $300,000 a year. However, the agency is supported by funds generated by the sale of property. Over half of the annual budget goes toward maintenance requirements. Maintenance levels are not considered adequate.

Contact.
Robert A. Volz, Executive Director
Land Utilization Authority
317 N. 11th Street, Room 800
St. Louis, Missouri 63101
(314) 621-7990

Objectives. To restore property to the tax rolls and to make land available to prospective buyers for in-city development.

Description. This authority was created by the state in 1974 to facilitate foreclosure and resale of tax-delinquent property. Its powers were first used in 1979. The county forecloses on tax-delinquent property and auctions it at a sheriff's sale. LRA bids (but does not immediately pay) the minimum amount at the sale, which is the amount of back taxes up to the time of foreclosure. If there is no higher bid, LRA is the successful bidder. It then looks for a buyer for the property. LRA does not confirm its purchase until a buyer has been found, and thus is only in possession of the parcel during the period that title is being transferred (generally two hours to one month). LRA activity acts as an incentive for purchase of marginal property, because LRA must only pay taxes accrued since the point of foreclosure, while other purchasers of property at the sheriff's sale pay all back taxes. The LRA does not take possession of property but serves only as a mechanism for its sale.

Accomplishments. Since LRA's inception, approximately 150 tax-delinquent properties have been sold. Of these, about 10 percent contained structures, while 25 lots were sold for new housing construction within the inner city. Public interest in and use of the mechanism is increasing. The program thus far has paid $75,000 in delinquent taxes to various taxing jurisdictions, more than repaying the $3,200 loan it received for start-up from Douglas County and the city of Omaha. Last year it cleared $5,000.

Costs. The program is administered out of the city planning department at no net cost to the city because staff salaries are more than covered in delinquent tax payments collected. Its largest costs are advertising ($450/year), liability insurance ($350/year), and recording deeds ($100/year).

Contact.
Mike Weese
City Planning Department
1819 Farnam Street
Omaha, Nebraska 68183
(402) 444-5206

Part II

Introduction

This part of the book discusses the research findings in greater detail than Part I. Chapter 4 looks at the quantity of infill land in each of the three case study counties, comparing the residential infill land supply with the demand for new housing over the next 10 years. Chapter 5 examines key characteristics of individual infill parcels from the perspective of the developer/builder—their size, location, zoning, physical limitations,j ownership, and availability. the nature and extent of those deterrents to infilling most frequently cited by real estate interests are reviewed. Cost comparisons of infill and fringe development in the three metropolitan areas are presented in Chapter 6.

These research findings are based on the results of three intensive case studies, conducted during 1979–1980 in the urbanized areas of Miami, Florida; Seattle, Washington; and Rochester, New York. Each case study involved examination of over 150 randomly selected vacant infill parcels, interviews with their owners, and examination of 40 to 50 developed infill parcels. RERC consulted with officials in nearly 20 cities, counties, and regional agencies who shared local experiences and data.

A wide spectrum of infill parcels was examined in the three case studies, ranging from lots suitable only for individual homes to bypassed tracts of 20 acres or more. For this study infill sites

- were located anywhere within the urbanized portion of the jurisdiction studied. (Cooperating local agencies defined the study area for each county under RERC guidance.)
- had water and sewer running to the property line or within a short distance of the site (no more than 1,000 feet). Parcels suitable for on-site water and sewer systems were also included (mainly found in Dade County).
- were of any size. However, parcels under 2,000 square feet were not subject to detailed investigation.
- could be in either public or private ownership. Permanent open space, parks, and playgrounds were excluded.
- were vacant or contained only temporary structures. Unused portions of large estates, government installations, business/institutional holdings, and parking lots were included to the extent that they could be identified as surplus.
- had no severe environmental constraints that would prohibit development. For example, land in the floodplain was included only if local regulations do not prohibit its development.
- could be zoned for any type of use—residential, commercial, or industrial.

The findings and conclusions presented here are based on stratified systematic samples of parcels identified as vacant in each county's tax assessment records. Using tax records was an efficient way of identifying ownership units (parcels), selecting a sample, and locating the owner.

It was determined early in the study that a sample of 150 would provide overall findings that would be reliable at 95 percent confidence level with an error range of ∓10 percent. Because the number of owners responding to opinion-type questions was small (usually around 50 in each case), confidence in these responses was much lower.

The information collected and processed for the vacant sampled sites was of three types: (1) hard information taken from official records, planning reports, maps, and earlier censuses or other socioeconomic data sources; (2) facts and opinions obtained through interviews with property owners or their representatives; and (3) observations noted during inspection of the sampled properties. All three types of information for the sampled properties in the case study were processed by computer.

Basic data collection instruments used in this research were:

- a physical, locational, and environmental data form used to record all parcel-specific information (from both secondary sources and visual inspections) for later computer entry
- interviews with owners of sampled vacant sites, designed to identify owner characteristics, ownership motives, development plans, perceived strengths and weaknesses of the site, and perceptions of government receptivity to development plans
- open-ended interviews with private sector respondents to assess regional market and regulatory context for infill development
- open-ended interviews with public sector respondents regarding infill policies, advantages and drawbacks, incentives, etc.

Additional sources were consulted in obtaining the data analyzed for the case studies. These included zoning and land use maps as well as local and federal maps covering soils, topography, and other physical conditions. Socioeconomic and demographic information was collected for census tracts with sample sites in order to expand upon perceptions of market strengths and weaknesses as voiced by property owners and "regional context" respondents. Sources used included the 1970 census and, where available, more recent small area estimates of population and households. These data were used to determine characteristics of census tracts and neighborhoods containing infill sites and how they compared with the county as a whole.

Infill Land Supply

The amount of infill land was estimated for each of the three case study locations and then discounted to reflect physical constraints, location problems in marketability, and the unwillingness of some owners to make their land available for development. The findings demonstrate the considerable variability among regions. In Dade and King Counties, the supply of available, marketable infill land was deemed insufficient to meet all of the residential demands of the 1980s. In Monroe County, the high potential residential infill land supply vastly exceeded probable needs for the decade. These findings are summarized in Figure 4-1.

Miami/Dade County

Dade County was selected as a case study to represent a large, rapidly growing metropolitan area. Between 1970 and 1978, its population grew at an average annual rate of 2.4 percent, from 1,268,000 to 1,528,000 persons. The population is expected to reach over 1.7 million by 1985. The county covers over 2,000 square miles, but much of the land in the western portion is either part of the Everglades National Park or in water conservation areas. Only 10 percent of the county land area is currently urbanized; however, the presence of sensitive lands to the west and the Atlantic Ocean on the east constrains the extent to which development can spread.

Dade County has a much larger multifamily housing stock than other rapidly growing metro areas in the Sunbelt. Apartments have been an accepted housing form for many years. Overall development patterns are more compact, for instance, than in Phoenix or Houston. Dade County is also unique among rapidly growing regions in its strong countywide planning functions. The county has established an urban growth boundary for 1985 that contains substantial quantities of

Figure 4-1
Residential Infill Land Supply, Case Study Counties
(Acreage rounded to nearest hundred)

	Miami (Dade Co.)	Seattle (King Co.)	Rochester (Monroe Co.)
Total vacant infill acres	36,500	70,000	65,800
Number of residentially zoned acres[1]	17,200	54,400	56,900
Number of residentially zoned parcels	17,300	32,300	13,500
Proportion with multiple physical/environmental limitations[2]	15%	7%	3%
Proportion deemed unavailable for development within five years	47%	50%	38%
Proportion with marketability limitations[3]	5%–10%	10%–15%	25%–30%
Net residential infill supply with strong potential			
Parcels	7,350	13,300	5,900
Acres	9,950	20,800	13,300
Projected demand for new housing, next 10 years	145,000[4]	116,000[5]	22,000[6]
Estimated land area needed (in acres)	12,000[4] 15,000	26,700[5]	5,700[7]

[1]Based on classifications contained in tax assessors' files, which do not always correspond with current zoning.
[2]Demonstrating two or more of the following conditions: below minimum single-family lot size with no adjacent vacant land; no direct road access; in 100-year floodplain; in slide hazard area; in wetlands area.
[3]In locations deemed unattractive due to adverse socioeconomic conditions and weak space markets.
[4]Regional Planning Council estimate for 1975–1985, extrapolated.
[5]Puget Sound Council of Governments estimate.
[6]Community Analysis Model estimate of household increases for 1980–1985, extrapolated.
[7]RERC estimate in the absence of local forecasts.

Infill parcel in Miami/Dade County.

unserved and partially served land that is not considered part of the infill land inventory. Development outside this boundary is strongly discouraged.

Developers are required to pay for all utility extensions. Because of this (and the fact that septic tanks and individual on-site wells have been permitted in many subdivisions within the urbanized area), there is relatively little preserviced vacant land in metropolitan Miami. The total supply is estimated at roughly 27,850 parcels (encompassing 36,500 acres), of which only 17,200 acres (47 percent) are residentially zoned. This amount must be further discounted for multiple physical or environmental limitations (affecting an estimated 15 percent of the residential parcels), market constraints (eliminating five percent to 10 percent), and sites that would not be made available within five years (47 percent according to interviews with their owners). This leaves approximately 7,350 residential parcels (covering 9,950 acres) with high potential for development.

The South Florida Regional Planning Council estimated an average annual demand for new housing of 14,500 dwelling units in the decade between 1975 and 1985 (3,700 single-family units and 10,800 multifamily). At currently typical densities, providing for 10 years' future housing demand at this annual rate would require 12,000–15,000 acres. It is easy to see that the residentially zoned infill land supply would be insufficient to meet this demand. In addition, closer examination of individual community zoning patterns shows an imbalance between the relative demand for single-family detached and multifamily housing and the amount of acreage zoned for each type of housing, especially in the suburbs.

Of the three case study counties, Dade County has the highest land requirements for future residential construction (despite the fact that three-fourths of its housing demand is for multifamily units); it also has the least amount of developable, available, and marketable residential infill acreage. The county's urban development

boundary must (and does) extend well beyond the currently urbanized area in order to allow an adequate supply of developable land for housing.

There is some evidence of overzoning for industrial uses in Dade County, which could limit the area's ability to absorb projected residential demands. Throughout Dade County, 12,000 acres of industrially zoned vacant land have been identified. Our research indicated that only 3,500 of these acres were fully served and within the already urbanized area, let alone available for development and free of environmental constraints.

Seattle/King County

King County was selected for this analysis as representative of a moderately growing urban region with a strong orientation toward growth management and environmental protection. Like Dade County, it has a total land area of roughly 2,100 square miles; more than half of the land area is located in the Cascade Mountains, much of it in national forests. King County's population grew from 1,159,375 to 1,264,991 between 1970 and 1980, or 9.1 percent. All of this growth occurred in the last half of the decade; the first half saw population losses because of layoffs in the aerospace industry. The population is expected to grow by 13.2 percent between 1980 and 1990.

In contrast to Dade County, multifamily housing in King County (especially multistory apartment buildings) is not as widely accepted; high-density development generally meets with resistance when proposed in both city and suburban neighborhoods.

Infill parcel in Seattle, Washington.

Both the county and the Puget Sound Council of Governments have adopted policies that promote growth management and infill development. Under state law, the county has defined areas where sewer service extensions would be permitted. Through its sewerage general plan, the county attempts to channel development into areas where public services already exist or are programmed; prime agricultural lands, floodways, and wetlands cannot be serviced. Much of the land within permitted service areas lacks full utilities, thus allowing for both new service extensions and infilling in already urbanized areas.

Over 38,000 vacant infill parcels (encompassing a total of 70,000 acres) can be found in urbanized King County. More than three-fourths of this acreage (85 percent of the parcels) is zoned for residential use, primarily for single-family homes and small-scale multifamily buildings. Similar to Dade County, the number of residential infill parcels in King County must be discounted by nearly 60 percent to account for sites with physical, marketability, or availability limitations, reflecting the results of the case study research. This leaves roughly 13,300 parcels with prime potential, covering 20,800 acres, or more than twice the supply estimated for Dade County.

The Puget Sound Council of Governments has projected a demand for roughly 66,000 new multifamily units and 50,000 single-family units between 1980 and 1990. At current densities, this would require over 3,000 multifamily acres and nearly 23,700 single-family acres. This indicates a closer match between supply and demand than in the Miami area, but still points to the fact that the current residential infill land supply will not be sufficient to accommodate the county's housing needs.

Rochester/Monroe County

Monroe County is a smaller and more slowly growing region than either of the other two case studies. Its 1980 population was 701,175, and it experienced a slight countywide population loss over the last decade (−1.5 percent). Its land area (675 square miles) is far smaller than either Dade County or King County, but it does not suffer from extensive physical or environmental constraints to development.

Extensive utility preservicing was a common practice in Monroe County in the last two decades. As a result, the developable infill land supply is extensive. However, the demand for vacant land, either within the urbanized area or at the urban fringe, is relatively weak for all land uses but industrial.

Little new housing has been built anywhere in the county in the last few years. The excess supply constructed in the early- to mid-1970s has only recently been absorbed. In light of the region's slow growth, developers are reluctant to begin new projects. Urban fringe land prices are low because of the depressed

Infill site in Rochester, New York.

market. New single-family housing at the fringe remains affordable and attractive to consumers, so Rochester area developers are reluctant to experiment with risky locations or innovative housing designs that might be more suitable for smaller infill lots.

It is estimated that urbanized Monroe County contains roughly 65,800 acres of fully served infill land—nearly as much as King County and 77 percent more than Dade County, both of which have much larger populations and total land areas. The vast majority of infill parcels in Monroe County are zoned residential, and virtually all of these are restricted to single-family use. Very little multifamily zoning exists outside the city of Rochester.

Relatively few sampled infill sites in Monroe County were subject to multiple physical or environmental constraints (three percent), and a smaller proportion was deemed unavailable for development by owners (38 percent) than in the other two cases. The average size of infill parcels in Monroe County was also larger than in either King or Dade County. However, anywhere from 25 percent to 30 percent of the sites would be limited in their marketability because of location. (These are primarily sites located within deteriorated neighborhoods in the city of Rochester.)

Nevertheless, the residential infill land supply with high potential in Monroe County appears to be more than adequate to handle the projected residential growth for the next 10 years. Nearly 13,300 such acres exist (in roughly 5,900 parcels). The demand for additional housing units is not likely to exceed 22,000 in the next decade. Even if the predominant single-family density pattern continues, this demand would at most require 5,700 acres.

Added Potential from Underutilized Land

In this analysis, infill land describes parcels that are totally vacant or contain temporary improvements, such as gravel paving on a parking lot. But when developers talk about infill projects, they usually refer to any building projects within the urbanized area—including projects involving demolition of existing buildings and redevelopment of the sites. Although not strictly infill, redevelopment projects offer many of the same advantages from the perspective of land resource conservation as do projects on purely vacant sites. However, redevelopment of underutilized land in urbanized areas will be at least as controversial as infill development, if only because redevelopment usually involves an increase in density, loss of structures that provided low-cost space, and reduced opportunities for rehabilitation and, in a few cases, historic preservation.

Because there is little agreement as to what constitutes underutilized land, there is no way to quantify how many such parcels exist, how many acres they cover in the aggregate, or how this amount compares with already vacant acreage. In reviewing the research of both regional planning groups and municipalities, a wide variety of definitions of underutilized land were identified. These include parcels:

- with abandoned buildings.
- containing occupied buildings, but with sufficient land to be further subdivided without changing the existing zoning (for example, a single home occupying a four-acre tract in an area zoned for ¼-acre lots). Figure 4-2 illustrates the potential for subdividing these large lots.
- zoned for a more intense use than that currently occupying the property (a multifamily site containing a single-family home).
- whose improvements are undervalued relative to the value of the land (a commercial parcel where the land is appraised at twice the value of the building).
- held by government agencies, religious groups, foundations, trusts, or railroads that can be deemed surplus but are not totally vacant.

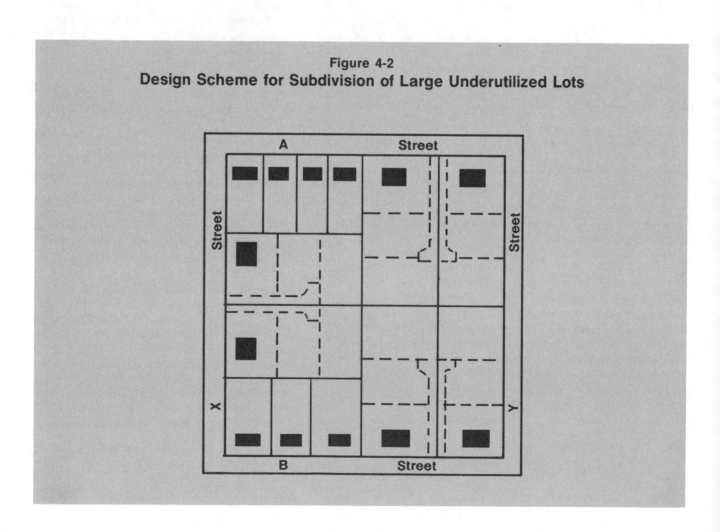

Figure 4-2
Design Scheme for Subdivision of Large Underutilized Lots

This is not to say that all, or even most, of these parcels should be redeveloped. Local policy may in fact encourage retention of such older buildings, especially when they can be rehabilitated at lower costs than new construction. Some cities are reexamining their zoning maps and downzoning certain parcels. This also encourages preservation of the existing low-cost housing stock by eliminating zoning as an incentive to demolition. Even when local governments want to encourage redevelopment, the private sector may not respond. Land in neighborhoods where abandoned buildings are already widespread will not be attractive, at least in the short run.

Despite the difficulties inherent in redevelopment of underutilized properties, they are often more attractive to builders than vacant infill sites. The city of Seattle noted that the majority of new multifamily units built in the city in the last few years involved some degree of demolition, usually of older single-family homes. This suggests that already vacant land suitable for condominiums and apartments was in short supply in the most desirable neighborhoods. Few cities have examined this phenomenon or determined its implications for local development policy.

Partial findings from the case studies indicate that underutilized land can be a considerable development resource. The city of Seattle indicates that over 19,000 net additional units could be built on sites that were occupied by single-family homes but zoned for multifamily use in 1980.[1] However, use of this capacity would not always be consistent with city policy, nor with existing Seattle ordinances that levy special fees on developers who demolish habitable housing units.

Underutilized land of a different type exists in the Seattle suburbs. King County estimated that there are over 20,000 partially developed single-family acres that could be further subdivided, over 80 percent of them in unincorporated areas.[2] Yet most of this acreage was not served by utilities; the existing housing uses individual septic and well systems. Whether owners would be willing to subdivide is another question. Persons who own vacant lots adjacent to their existing homes are not always eager to make them available for development. The same is likely to hold true for homeowners whose large lots are partially developed and could theoretically be subdivided.

In the Dade and Monroe County cases, tax rolls were examined to determine the number of parcels where assessed values of land exceeded improvement values. In Monroe County, only 3,200 such parcels were identified.

[1] City of Seattle, Office of Policy and Evaluation, *Mayor's Recommended Multifamily Land Use Policies: Final EIS* (July 1980), p. 95.
[2] King County, Division of Planning, *Vacant Land Inventory* (1979).

In Dade County, there were over 45,000 such parcels, which contrasts with the relative scarcity of purely vacant land in the Miami area.

Again, determining whether these properties can or should be cleared and redeveloped requires site-specific analyses and discussions with local officials and developers. What can be concluded is that underutilized land is an important supplement to the vacant infill land supply. Many larger projects will, of necessity, require a combination of infilling and redevelopment, if only because infill sites tend to be smaller than those typically used at the urban fringe.

Amplification from Other Research

There are no infill land supply/demand analyses from other metropolitan areas that use the same methodology as the above case studies, but related research efforts have produced findings that amplify this analysis.

Officials of the Association of Bay Area Governments, which covers the San Francisco region, stated that their housing growth forecasts for the year 2000 exceed the capacity of vacant "prime developable" residential land— vacant land designated for residential development under local plans and capital improvement programs. Most of this acreage cannot be defined strictly as infill land because it lacked full services. As in Dade County, the shortage of residential land was attributed, in part, to overzoning for industrial uses.[3] Regionwide, only 36 percent of the vacant land set aside for industry in 1975 was projected to be needed within the next 20 years.

In contrast, regional planners in the Albany, New York, area believe that as of 1978 vacant land with sewers could accommodate over 61,000 dwelling units, whereas regional growth forecasts at the time indicated household growth of only 32,400 by 1985. In the city of Albany itself, vacant land could accommodate 7,800 units, and the 1980–1985 demand forecast was for only 1,950. The disparities were even greater in the city of Schenectady and in certain older suburbs.[4]

The Twin Cities Metro Council (Minneapolis-St. Paul) tracks the supply of vacant land within its urbanized area as part of its ongoing growth management program. The region has a "large oversupply" of serviced land as a result of widespread sewer extension programs of the 1960s and slowing growth rates. This land supply is well distributed

[3] Rune Carlson to Real Estate Research Corporation, dated April 18, 1980.
[4] Capital District Regional Planning Commission, "Local Development Capacity Profile," Chapter IV in *Regional Housing Element: Dimensions of Needs Analysis and Plan Implementation* (June 1979).

throughout the metro area. As a result, the Council has designated rural areas where urban sewer and transportation services will not be permitted until at least 1990.[5]

Monitoring land supply to assure that growth management programs do not create artificial shortages was also the goal of the Metropolitan Service District vacant land inventory, which covered the four-county Portland, Oregon, region. Over 119,000 vacant acres were identified within the urban growth boundary in 1977, of which roughly half were zoned for residential use and 13 percent were zoned for commercial and industrial use. The balance was located in floodplains or on steep slopes (nearly 22,000 acres).[6] The inventory did not distinguish between land with full utility service and unserved land, though this distinction was contemplated for future updates. Nor were attempts made to compare supply with demand, nor to determine availability. (The latter deficiency is true of all regional vacant land inventories reviewed as part of this project.)

Colorado Springs reported that 42 percent of the land within the city limits was vacant, amounting to 28,000–30,000 acres. Officials believe that this supply is sufficient to handle demand to the year 2005.[7] The city of Dallas indicated that there were 1,300 acres of vacant land in the inner city that could accommodate 13,390 new dwelling units, of which 9,750 would be multifamily.[8] The overall density of development, consistent with current zoning and development patterns, would be 10 units per acre.

Characterizing Regional Infill Potential

Variation in the extent of infill opportunities among regions makes it difficult to generalize as to the potential for directing future growth to infill sites. In many ways, the three case studies are representative of other similar regions—rapidly growing or declining; environmentally fragile or with limited constraints; strong or weak central city markets; physically compact or spread out. But in other ways, each metropolitan area is unique and must be analyzed independently. In all cases, economic considerations will be paramount to infill potential.

Growing regions probably offer the greatest opportunity for encouraging consideration of infill sites. Infill development will become increasingly attractive—if it is not already so—as fringe land prices escalate in growing regions. In many regions with stagnant or declining population bases, the exurban land market is actually weakening.

Both King and Dade Counties are examples of growing regions without extensive preservicing where developers must pay for interceptor and water main extensions needed for their projects. In both cases, however, there are officially designated "growth boundaries" or limits on utility extensions. An ample supply of unserviced land to allow for further urbanization will be needed as the region grows. However, they do not permit proliferation of new subdivisions on demand throughout the county, and they coordinate public capital improvement programs to support orderly growth.

Slow growing regions are generally experiencing severe fiscal constraints. Thus, their need for infilling is pressing, but the economics are less favorable, especially for central city projects. Land at the fringe is usually inexpensive relative to land in the city or the more attractive close-in suburbs, and there may even be preserviced vacant land on the edge of the metropolitan area. The lowest priced urban land is often in low-income neighborhoods where existing buildings have not been well maintained. In smaller regions like Rochester/ Monroe County, auto commuting times from the urban fringe to major employment centers are still under one-half hour and mass transit systems are not well developed. Private developers in these regions do not see

---

[5] See Twin Cities Metro Council, *Development Framework: Policy, Plan Program* (September 1975).

[6] Ray Bartlett, "Developable Land Supply and Demand Monitoring System in the Portland Metropolitan Area," in *Urban Land Markets: Price Indices, Supply Measures, and Public Policy Effects* (Washington, D.C.: ULI–the Urban Land Institute, 1980).

[7] City of Colorado Springs, "A Resolution Establishing Urban Infill Policy." Adopted April 14, 1980.

[8] City of Dallas, Department of Housing and Urban Rehabilitation. "Infilling Potential in the Dallas Inner City " (Draft report, undated).

strong reasons for undertaking riskier infill projects when fringe opportunities are extensive and the economics of building at the fringe make more sense.

The importance of local market conditions cannot be overemphasized in evaluating infill potential. Market conditions are highly localized, varying significantly among neighborhoods and among parcels within neighborhoods. Even in a rapidly growing region like Phoenix, some city neighborhoods are not currently attracting developer interest. Phoenix examined a number of inner city infill parcels and found that they remained vacant primarily because of high asking prices for the land, inappropriate zoning (and the high time and fee costs in processing zoning changes), deteriorated neighborhood conditions, or owners unwilling to sell.[9]

Conversely, even in regions where infill potential is relatively weak overall, certain locations will attract investment; developers will need relatively little in the way of public inducements or incentives to consider these sites.

---

[9] City of Phoenix, *Infill Committee Report* (Prepared for the Mayor and City Council, February 14, 1980).

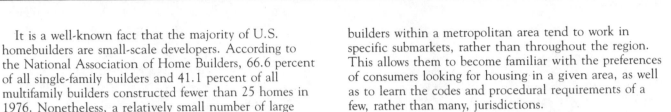

It is a well-known fact that the majority of U.S. homebuilders are small-scale developers. According to the National Association of Home Builders, 66.6 percent of all single-family builders and 41.1 percent of all multifamily builders constructed fewer than 25 homes in 1976. Nonetheless, a relatively small number of large regional and national builders are responsible for much of the single-family residential development activity at the suburban fringe. Firms building over 100 homes a year accounted for only 8.1 percent of all builders, but 61.6 percent of all units in 1976.

Many large builders are unfamiliar with the nature of scattered sites and how to work successfully with them. They express concern that working on small disparate sites will mean diseconomies of scale; they are also worried about delays occasioned by neighborhood opposition and lengthy approval times for infill projects. As Figure 5-1 indicates, few large builders are involved with scattered sites, though 38 percent of the builders who construct fewer than 10 units a year work exclusively with scattered sites.

The typical suburban tract developer (who both subdivides land and constructs homes—some presold and some on a speculative basis) usually looks for at least 20 acres and, more often, 40 or more for a conventional subdivision. Relatively few infill parcels are of this size, even if the assembly potential of adjacent vacant lots is taken into account.

Smaller builders who typically work on scattered sites will not automatically be attracted to infill projects. Many are custom builders. Others work only on finished lots that they buy from developers. Moreover, most small builders within a metropolitan area tend to work in specific submarkets, rather than throughout the region. This allows them to become familiar with the preferences of consumers looking for housing in a given area, as well as to learn the codes and procedural requirements of a few, rather than many, jurisdictions.

Many builders believe that it is harder to work in central cities than in suburban or rural communities; this belief may persist even in areas where city governments have made a conscious effort at improving relations with the construction industry by streamlining their approval processes, providing development expediters, etc. Although we found that the bulk of infill acreage is located in suburbs, many suburban jurisdictions see no reason to encourage infill activity—especially if it involves attached housing or higher densities. City governments may be more receptive to proposals from infill builders.

Yet infill building is occurring in many cities and older suburbs. To date, infilling is perceived as being done primarily by individual entrepreneurs. In metropolitan Seattle, infill builders are often part-time contractors and tradesmen who work on these projects in their spare time. As occurred with rehabilitation in the mid-1970s, an industry has evolved to meet the demand.

There has been little evidence of interest in infilling on the part of the big national and regional builders (those who typically construct over 500 units per year). However there are signs that this too is changing. Interviews with representatives of 52 of the nation's largest building/development companies conducted by

Figure 5-1
Number of Separate Construction Locations in 1976, by Number of Units Started
(In percentages)

Number of Separate Locations	Total, All Builders	By Units Started in 1976					
		Less than 10	10–25	26–50	51–100	101–500	501 and Over
1	17.3	17.1	18.6	20.3	22.7	11.8	26.7
2–3	34.9	20.9	37.1	38.0	46.4	43.0	20.0
4–5	14.6	10.7	17.0	20.3	21.8	16.1	13.3
6–8	5.5	3.0	4.7	4.8	5.5	17.2	26.7
9 or more	2.0	1.5	3.1	1.6	—	4.3	13.3
Scattered lots only	25.7	37.8	19.5	15.0	3.6	7.5	—

Source: Sumichrast, et al. *Profile of the Builder.* (Washington, DC: National Association of Home Builders, 1979), Table 38.

Real Estate Research Corporation in 1980 revealed that 58 percent of the respondents' firms considered infill development projects in 1979.[1]

Location

Private developers have not actively pursued infill projects because infill land is commonly believed to be concentrated in lower-income inner city neighborhoods. When interviews were conducted with builders and lenders in the Rochester, New York, area at the start of the case study research, they identified infill land as synonymous with large urban renewal tracts that had been cleared by the city of Rochester 10 or more years ago. Little thought was given to the far greater supply of skipped-over acreage in the suburban towns. Respondents expressed surprise when shown computer printouts and maps pinpointing the location of vacant tracts in the close-in suburbs or in stable middle-income neighborhoods in the city of Rochester.

Infill sites can be found in virtually all city neighborhoods. A portion of the total inventory may be clustered in low-income areas. This is especially true in older core locations where structure deterioration or fire damage has led to widespread demolition. Such concentrations were observed in both Rochester and Miami, but not in Seattle. Developers are rightly concerned about their ability to develop infill sites in low-income neighborhoods. In the absence of sufficient subsidies limiting the concentration of assisted housing in low-income neighborhoods, new housing will be infeasible for most of these sites. Circumstances in every city will be different depending on the age of existing buildings, past

maintenance efforts, and quality of construction, as well as socioeconomic conditions. (See Figure 5-2.)

Infill parcels in the suburbs were also found to be larger than parcels in the central cities and were more likely to be deemed available for development by their owners. (See Figure 5-3.) As a result, the majority of infill only projects may well be built in the suburbs, whereas new investment opportunities in the central cities will more likely involve a combination of techniques—rehabilitation, demolition, and infilling.

Owners of available infill parcels who were interviewed as part of the case studies rated the neighborhoods in which their parcels were located very positively, as summarized in Figure 5-4. The table also includes data from a similar survey conducted in metropolitan Albany, New York, by the Capital District Regional Planning Commission.

In all cases but Albany, the majority of respondents believed that their properties were located in areas with high degrees of current investment activity or in stable neighborhoods. Fewer than 20 percent of the sites were believed to be in unattractive locations. Owners with available sites also were positive about the current market for their vacant land.

Owners were also asked how they thought the market for infill land would change in the next five years. Their responses are presented in Figure 5-5. Respondents from the Rochester and Albany regions were the least optimistic. In contrast, only a few property owners in King County felt that the market would weaken; they attributed this to rapidly escalating prices, not locational problems.

[1] Real Estate Research Corporation, *Emerging Trends in Real Estate: 1981*, prepared for The First National Bank of Chicago (1980). Data taken from unpublished working papers.

Figure 5-2
Sampled Infill Parcels and Acreage by City/Suburban Location
(In percentages)

	Miami (Dade County)	Seattle (King County)	Rochester (Monroe County)
Central City			
Parcels	28*	41	47
Acreage	2*	5	3
Suburbs			
Parcels	72	59	53
Acreage	98	95	97

Notes:
*Includes both Miami and Miami Beach.

Figure 5-3
Sample Parcels Available by Location
(In percentages)

Dade County		King County		Monroe County	
Miami/Miami Beach	41	Seattle	44	Rochester	57
Suburbs	58	Suburbs	56	Suburbs	65

Figure 5-4
Owners' Characterization of Neighborhood
Surrounding Sampled Vacant Infill Parcels
(In percentages)

Neighborhood Characterization	Miami (Dade County)	Seattle (King County)	Rochester (Monroe County)	Albany, New York Urbanized Area
	(N = 44)	(N = 55)	(N = 81)	(N = 2)
Area of major investment and development activity	28	51	28	24
Stable area—little new construction occurring	24	21	31	19
Area with past problems but good long-range potential	19	9	14	52
Area generally considered unattractive for new development	9	8	16	0
Did not know/not applicable	20	11	10	5

Figure 5-5
Owners' Assessment of Change in the
Market for Infill Land, Next Five Years
(In percentages)

Five-Year Market Projection	Miami (Dade County)	Seattle (King County)	Rochester, New York (Monroe County)	Albany, New York Urbanized Area
	(N = 44)	(N = 53)	(N = 74)	(N = 27)
Will improve	82	74	49	60
Will stay the same	16	9	34	15
Will weaken	0	8	0	0
Not sure	2	9	18	25

Because owners of vacant properties may not always be well informed about market conditions, independent assessments of key physical and socioeconomic characteristics affecting sampled sites were made by RERC. Our observations again confirmed that most infill sites are located in well-maintained residential neighborhoods or industrial areas. In all three cases, fewer than 10 percent of the sites examined were located in areas with poor street conditions (needing repair or rebuilding). Cleanliness of streets and public areas was rated poor in fewer than 10 percent of the locations in King and Dade Counties, and in only 18 percent of the cases in Monroe County (largely within the city of Rochester). Abandoned buildings were observed near 31 percent of the Monroe County sites (53 percent in the city; 12 percent in the suburbs), but such buildings were near only four percent of the Dade County sites and 12 percent of the King County sites.

Size of Infill Parcels

A frequently cited drawback in using infill land is the small size of typical parcels. The 40-acre residential tract or the 120 acres needed for a modern industrial park are rarely found within already urbanized areas. As a result, the economies of scale and greater certainty and control that accompany development of large tracts are not possible.

On the other hand, consumer requirements are changing; expectations are being downsized. Affordability means accepting smaller dwelling units and greater overall densities. Quality space on smaller land areas can be achieved with creative design and innovative construction techniques. Examples of successful, small-scale infill projects exist in almost every metropolitan area. (See inset.) Large development organizations may have to

adapt their procedures, but they can reorganize to build small projects in several locations simultaneously. And greater skills can be fostered among smaller builders willing to work with infill sites.

Developers are correct when they state that most passed-over parcels are small. In the King County case study, half of the sampled tax parcels are under ¼-acre—the lot size of a typical middle-income suburban tract house. In Dade and Monroe Counties, six of 10 parcels fall below this standard. As a result, the likelihood of significant industrial or commercial activity on infill sites is not great. In the absence of large land areas, residential construction will be the predominant use for vacant acreage. Some land will also be absorbed for convenience retailing in underserved markets and for service businesses and professional offices.

Changing tastes and creative design make many previously overlooked parcels buildable, but there are size thresholds that establish realistic parameters for infill opportunities. The lower limits, which could "disqualify" a site for development, are different for each land use. The parcel size challenges facing the infill builder are suggested by Figure 5-6. It provides a basis for matching the land requirements of various activities against the availability of different sized parcels of vacant land.

Uses of Infill Land

It appears that there will be few opportunities for meaningful industrial development on skipped-over parcels. In Miami's Dade County, the tiny size of properties already zoned for this use would preclude most manufacturing, distribution, or other industrial activities. The outlook is scarcely more optimistic in the other two case study counties, where the median industrially zoned parcel is far less than an acre in size.

Freestanding industrial facilities are rapidly being replaced by planned industrial parks as the preferred site for new plants and facilities. As many as two-thirds of new industrial facilities are now locating in planned parks where a company can purchase or lease land without the problems of obtaining permits or taking on expensive land development activity. Small firms, in particular, enjoy the benefits of locating in industrial parks.

This parcel of nearly five acres is atypical of the size of most bypassed sites.

Oak Street Rowhouses
Portland, Oregon

The metropolitan area of Portland, Oregon, is by far the largest city in Oregon, with over 1.2 million people in 1980. Not as rapidly growing as many other western cities, Portland nevertheless increased in population by roughly 20 percent during the 1970s, and the city exhibits a broad range of impressive recent developments in the downtown and outlying areas.

The Oak Street Rowhouses, completed in June 1980, are located in a turn-of-the-century residential, commercial, and light industrial area of Portland. They appeal to a broad range of people. Owners typically have incomes from $15,000 to $25,000, and include retired, singles, and families with children.

The area is about a mile east of the Willamette River, which separates this part of the city from downtown. The site area itself is 18,000 square feet, slightly smaller than half of a city block, divided into 10 1,800-square-foot units. Net project density is 24 units per acre, excluding streets. Since the site is a few feet higher in elevation than surrounding streets, it was possible to excavate the site so the garages are at "basement" level, while the main level is still at grade. Garages are of generous size, providing ample space for workshops or storage in addition to a car.

The 10-unit development consists of two back-to-back buildings, each facing the street. Private, fenced courtyards behind each building open onto a community lawn area, which includes two vegetable gardens. The two-story frame buildings have pitched roofs, front porches, and siding and exterior materials that are reminiscent of neighboring houses.

There are two basic unit plans. Six units offer 1,345 square feet of living space (excluding garage area), with three bedrooms. Four units have 1,108 square feet, with two bedrooms. All units have a half-bath on the main floor and a full bath at the bedroom level. Bay windows, skylights, combined living-dining rooms, plus small breakfast areas in kitchens provide a sense of openness. Passive solar space heating is supplemented by gas-fired forced-air heating and a wood-burning stove. Energy-saving features include double-glazed windows, R-19 insulation at walls, and R-30 insulation at attics. Awnings above windows permit occupants to control the amount of sunlight.

The purchase price for each unit ranged from $55,000 to $65,000. The developer paid $55,000 for the site. Construction costs were $38 per square foot of living area. All of the units were presold. A homeowners' association manages the development.

Since the dwelling units were presold, owners were able to participate in the development process, thereby saving about 10 to 15 percent of the sales price. The owner group, for example, performed all the legwork required to secure permits and to satisfy local regulations. The developer believes that the owner's efforts were by far the important factor in reducing development costs.

After neighborhood groups had successfully opposed a proposed development of 18 townhouses, the vacant half-block was acquired by a group of people who wished to own homes in the area. Working closely with the neighborhood association, the new group was able to win approval for a conditional use permit, which allowed 10 units instead of seven on the site area. The developer was required to provide some additional amenities. The process took about 20 months from initial land option to completion of the project.

Developer:	Oak Street Development Group 1313 S.E. Oak Street Portland, OR 97214
Architects:	Andrews Architects 728 S.E. 11th Street Portland, OR 97214
Engineering:	Kramer-Gehlen Associates Vancouver, Washington
Landscaping:	Whitmore Associates Portland, Oregon

Oak Street rowhouses.

Figure 5-6
Median Size of Sampled Vacant Tax Parcels
(Median parcel size in square feet)

Zoning Designation	Miami (Dade County)	Seattle (King County)	Rochester, N.Y. (Monroe County)
Single-Family	8,600	10,000	10,400
Multifamily	6,500	10,900	3,800
Commercial	6,500	7,700	5,900
Industrial	7,000	30,600	24,500

A recent survey indicates that industrial parks range in size from 16 to over 10,000 acres.[2] The average size is just under 300 acres, with 30 percent between 20 and 60 acres. (Industrial park observers believe that smaller parks will predominate in the future.) Within planned parks, individual parcels are typically quite small. More than 60 percent of the sites surveyed were between ½ acre and three acres.

Commercial land uses are difficult to characterize. They range from semi-portable hot dog stands to regional shopping malls of half a million square feet or more. Office structures may be small buildings on lots of less than 5,000 square feet or full square block edifices. Movie theaters, banks, gas stations, and scores of other activities all fall within the general category of commercial land use. In terms of land coverage, neighborhood retail strip centers anchored by a supermarket are a city's major commercial land users. Commercially zoned parcels usually cluster tightly around major intersections and along arterials.

The diverse commercial sector offers infill potential, but the case study data reveal that such use will be limited. The typical size of commercially zoned tax parcels does not reach even ¼ acre in any of the three counties. Many of the properties are currently used for ancillary parking for various nearby retail or service businesses. Given their small size, this may be their highest and best use unless they can be assembled with other adjacent and nearby parcels in a redevelopment effort.

Convenience retail uses are the most probable commercial infill activities. This will be especially true in areas of high or increasing density where few parking spaces are required.

Small vacant parcels are best suited to residential development. In fact, most of the infill parcels are zoned for single family or multifamily housing.

Current U.S. Department of Commerce figures reveal that the median lot size for single-family homes is shrinking. The typical site was 9,870 square feet in 1977 and 9,580 in 1979.[3] In the three case studies, sampled infill parcels that are zoned for single-family housing have a median size of about 10,000 square feet in King County and in Monroe County, with a somewhat smaller typical lot size in the Miami area. (See Figure 5-6.)

By itself, parcel size does not present an obstacle to residential infill development. The vacant sites in most locations are easily large enough to accommodate single-family dwellings. Impediments to large volumes of single-family infill construction relate more to the fact that, for many developers, scattered small lots are more costly or time consuming to build on than a large tract that is subdivided and built out in a coordinated fashion. As discussed earlier, scattered building requires dealing with more public agencies and understanding more submarkets than most builders have coped with in the past. Perhaps more important is that individual lots in good neighborhoods tend to be very expensive for single houses. Rezoning for duplex or townhouse designs may be inappropriate, given the character of surrounding homes, and may be difficult to obtain even when such styles do not conflict with existing neighborhood character.

The outlook for multifamily projects is also mixed. The figures in Figure 5-6 show that the typical parcel already zoned for attached housing in both Dade and Monroe Counties is larger than a single-family lot but still very small. Most are suitable for duplexes or townhouses. Few parcels are large enough to provide for the multistory apartment or condominium complexes that were typically built in the suburbs in the 1960s and early 1970s.

Parcel size, along with zoning and the property owners' unwillingness to make land available, is one of the fundamental dimensions along which realistic infill feasibility must be measured. Without land assembly and demolition, infill development at any scale will be largely limited to single-family or small-scale attached housing.

---

[2] Whaeler, Van C. "See How They Grow: A Survey of Industrial Park Development Trends," *Industrial Development*, July/August 1978, pp. 13–14.

[3] U.S. Department of Commerce Construction Reports, Series C25-79-13, *Characteristics of New Housing: 1979* (August 1980).

Residential infill development in Seattle.

Industrial and commercial development will be the exceptional case, rather than a major focus of activity. Large apartment complexes are likely to be buildable on only a very small number of parcels.

Land Assembly

A vacant infill parcel is a legally defined ownership unit that may be adjacent to or surrounded by other similarly vacant properties. If this is the case, a larger area may be assembled from two or more contiguous parcels.

In King and Monroe Counties, between 50 percent and 60 percent of the sampled vacant infill parcels were observed to be adjacent to other vacant land. Properties in the city were just as likely as suburban parcels to be part of a larger area of vacant land. The data in Figure 5-7 indicates that residential parcels in these two cases

were somewhat less likely than commercial and industrial tracts to be located next to another unused piece of land, but the difference is not great. In Dade County, the infill sites were slightly more isolated, with only 40 percent bordered by another undeveloped property. Sites in the cities of Miami and Miami Beach were far less likely to have land assembly potential than suburban sites. Differences by zoning were insignificant in Dade County.

Land assembly involves more than determining the physical proximity of two pieces of land. What appears to be a large tract may be subdivided and in the hands of multiple owners. Identifying and contacting owners and then bringing several properties into single ownership is a time-consuming and potentially expensive process. Unfortunately, only 18 percent of the infill owners in Dade and King Counties (but 35 percent in Monroe County) report that they own vacant property adjacent to the sampled parcels. This means that consolidating infill parcels into more easily developable units will, in more cases, demand coordinated land assembly involving multiple owners.

Ownership and Availability of Infill Land

The question of who owns vacant parcels within the urbanized area is of critical concern to potential developers and to public agencies. Of greater practical importance is the issue of whether these owners are willing to develop their land or make it available for development by others. If land is not available, it is important to understand why—and whether anything can or should be done to encourage owners to change their attitudes. Many reasons are typically given for why infill land remains vacant. Individual owners may maintain vacant land for their own personal use. Businesses and government agencies frequently hold onto unused parcels

Figure 5-7
Land Assembly Potential
(Percentage of all sampled sites)

	Miami (Dade County)	Seattle (King County)	Rochester (Monroe County)
Presence of Vacant Land Adjacent to Sample Parcels	40	52	57
Central City	16	53	57
Suburbs	50	51	56
Single-Family	43	45	47
Multifamily	44	53	61
Commercial/Industrial/ Other	39	59	64
Owners Who Indicate They Own Adjacent Vacant Parcels	18	18	35

117

to accommodate ancillary or temporary operations—parking or storage—or for long-term future facility needs. Developers and local officials also believe that a significant number of bypassed sites are withheld from the market in anticipation of continued appreciation in value.

Almost half of the parcels sampled in the three study areas are not now available for development, nor will they be in the next five years. This lack of interest in making vacant land available may represent the most important single barrier to infill activity.

Infill landowners are typically portrayed as speculators, as absentee or foreign owners, and as large-scale real estate interests. The case study findings refute this perception. Approximately half of the vacant parcels were held by private individuals. Another 15 to 25 percent were under the control of government agencies, including such public entities as school districts, renewal agencies, or state universities. The remaining 25 to 35 percent were in the hands of business partnerships, corporations, or nonprofit institutions. Parcels owned by businesses were larger than those held by individuals in all three case studies.

Little other research has been done on the ownership of vacant urban land, but similar results were found in Albany, New York. In that region, 62 percent of a sample of undeveloped properties were found to be owned by individuals, 28 percent by businesses, and the remainder (10 percent) by government agencies.

The landholdings of individual owners were generally zoned for single-family residential uses. Many of these were vacant lots that belong to the owner of the house next door. Not surprisingly, businesses were more likely to own the larger vacant tracts and the land zoned for commercial and industrial use. However, it is interesting to note that most of the sampled multifamily parcels in Monroe County were government owned. Multifamily zoned land is scarce in the Rochester area; what little exists is primarily in urban renewal or tax-delinquent sites controlled by the city of Rochester.

In general, government ownership of infill land appears to be more significant within central cities than in suburban areas. Government-owned land accounted for over 20 percent of the sampled sites in the city of Seattle but only 10 percent of the suburban sites. Over 90 percent of the government-owned parcels in the Monroe County sample were located inside the city of Rochester. Other central cities evidence similar concentrations of publicly owned land, especially where tax delinquency is widespread or large-scale urban renewal programs were undertaken. For example, 20 of 90 sampled infill lots in

the city of Wilmington, Delaware, were found to be under government control.[4] Although Washington, D.C., is not typical of most cities, research on its vacant land ownership found 21 percent of all vacant parcels over ½ acre in size to be owned by federal and local government agencies, and five percent owned by foreign nations.[5] The Albany region found that just over one-fifth of the city parcels it sampled were owned by urban renewal authorities. Again, though, the pattern can vary significantly among regions.

There was little out-of-town ownership of urban vacant land. Absentee ownership by large corporations or by foreign investors was a rare phenomenon. This makes sense: foreign investors and domestic corporations are more interested in income-producing properties than in holding vacant land (especially small parcels) for future appreciation or in undertaking a risky and politically sensitive program of land development.

Several jurisdictions that have examined infill land have also discovered that owners of passed-over property live in the locality. A study in Montgomery County, Pennsylvania, revealed that only two of 128 vacant landowners did not live in that jurisdiction. In King County, where there is a common perception that Canadian corporations and real estate interests control large areas of land, nine out of 10 surveyed owners resided within the metropolitan area.

Most infill parcels were not, as is commonly believed, controlled by people who make their living in the real estate business. The majority of private sector infill landowners—both individuals and businesses—were not actively involved in real estate as developers, builders, or brokers.

Infill vs. Suburban Fringe Ownership Patterns

Additional perspective on ownership patterns and motives is afforded by a comparison with the findings of a recent analysis of landholding at the urban fringe—the area in-between active agricultural uses and intensive suburban subdivision activity. Six metropolitan areas were studied: four in the U.S. and two in Canada. Sponsored by the Lincoln Institute of Land Policy, this study found that 85 percent of urban fringe parcels in the U.S. regions were owned by individuals, representing over two-thirds of the total land area. The remaining acreage was owned by family businesses, partnerships, and

[4] City of Wilmington, Department of Planning, *Vacant Lot Inventory* (1979).

[5] District of Columbia, Legislative Commission on Housing, *Vacant Land in the District of Columbia and Its Immediate Housing Development Potential* (July 1978).

Figure 5-8
Land Ownership Patterns at the
Suburban Fringe; Four Metro Areas*

	Percent of Parcels Owned	Percent of Land Area Owned
Individuals	85	69
Family businesses	8	13
Partnerships	3	8
Corporations	4	10
Other	0	1

*Atlanta, Boston, Buffalo, and Sacramento.

Source: Brown, et al. *Land Ownership and Market Dynamics at the Urban Periphery: Implications for Land Policy Design and Implementation.* Prepared for Lincoln Institute of Land Policy (June 1980). Based on interviews with 700 landowners.

other corporate entities, as shown in Figure 5-8. Among the sampled infill parcels, the proportion owned by individuals was significantly less, about 50 percent of the parcels as opposed to 85 percent in the outlying areas.

The Lincoln Institute study characterized fringe landowners as users, investors, and developers. Fully 75 percent of the parcels were owned by persons using their land as farm or as rural dwellings. Another 19 percent were characterized as investors who were holding the land in the hope of realizing value appreciation upon sale as the potential for urban use increased. Only six percent were actually developers, although developers tended to own larger parcels than did the other two owner groups. Like infill land, fringe land was characterized by long-term ownership, especially among users (half had held their land for more than 20 years, while half of the developers purchased their land after 1970).

Why Owners Hold Vacant Land

To better understand the reason for holding infill parcels, owners of parcels in the case study samples were asked why they maintain ownership of vacant sites. The most frequently encountered response was that the land represents an investment. This was not surprising given the number of private owners holding multiple parcels. However, a significant number reported that the property was held for business, personal, or family use. There were many owners who held vacant lots next to their homes or businesses and "used" the land simply as extra open space; they were not planning to sell or to build on it.

Government agencies, including local school systems, were frequently found to hold land in the public trust against future facility needs or to provide open space. As long as a valid public purpose was being served, there was no overriding reason for these parcels to be sold or leased for development.

Investment appreciation was a powerful motive for both individual and business owners, as is seen in Figure 5-9. Such properties are likely to be available for development in the long run, given positive market conditions, available financing, and "the right price." Sites acquired for personal use were generally not on the market; most of these owners would not sell to others regardless of price. The same can be said for businesses or institutions that deliberately bought excess land to provide for future expansion; this land may remain vacant for a long time before it is needed.

In addition, there are negative reasons why individuals and firms retained possession of vacant acreage. In Rochester, New York, for example, a faltering economy and rapid suburbanization created a large supply of tax-delinquent properties inside the city, as well as properties held by lending institutions because of mortgage defaults. Legal or tax entanglements in selling a piece of land frequently caused owners to retain a property they might just as soon dispose of. Restrictive zoning, the opposition of neighborhood and community groups, and poor market conditions (including the nonavailability and high costs of financing) also contributed to keeping infill parcels undeveloped. Market weakness may be reflected in the number of projects that were proposed for sampled vacant sites but then "fell through." Of those properties for which there were no current development plans, 10 percent in Dade County and 12 percent in King County indicated prior interest in development that did not proceed; this was true for 25 percent of the Monroe County sites.

119

Figure 5-9
Proportion of Private Owners
Citing Various Motives for Holding Infill Land
(Multiple responses were possible)

Motives and Type of Owner	Miami (Dade County)	Seattle (King County)	Rochester (Monroe County)
Future appreciation/investment			
Individuals	37%	58%	29%
Businesses and institutions	22	48	22
Personal use			
Individuals	35	35	39
Businesses and institutions	4	0	11
Future expansion space			
Individuals	15	8	5
Businesses and institutions	14	13	7
Parking area			
Individuals	14	9	15
Businesses and institutions	39	19	30

Owners of vacant urban land in the Albany area offered a similar variety of responses when asked why their property remained vacant. The most frequently cited reasons were:

- holding land for future development or sale (25 percent)
- previous efforts at selling were unsuccessful (12 percent)
- financing for development was hard to obtain (10 percent)
- land was held for owner's personal use (eight percent)
- zoning was too restrictive (eight percent)
- neighborhood opposed development (eight percent)
- title problem—owner recently deceased (eight percent).

Owners were asked whether they intended to make their infill property available for development within the next five years. Slightly more than half of the sampled lots—51 percent in King County, 54 percent in Dade County, and 62 percent in Monroe County—were being planned for development or would be available for sale or lease within five years. In the Albany study, 63 percent of the sites had development plans or were for sale. Conversely, however, as many as half of the parcels that would appear to be potential infill sites were unlikely to be developed without an attempt to change the current thinking of property owners.

Physical Conditions of Infill Sites

As would be expected, environmental constraints on infill parcels vary tremendously from one region to another. For example, 57 percent of the vacant infill sites sampled in urbanized Dade County (Miami) were located wholly or partially within the 100-year floodplain, but this was true of only eight percent of the parcels in the Seattle case and six percent in Rochester. On the other hand, landslide hazards associated with steep slope development affected 13 percent of the sample sites in the Seattle area (and an even greater proportion within the city of Seattle itself) and 43 percent of the vacant residential land in the city of Portland, Oregon.[6] Some of the most attractive and creative infill projects involved hillside land that was considered too expensive to develop (and hence was skipped over) years ago. The improved market for infilling in places like Seattle or Portland has made the extra investment required for sloping sites worthwhile.

Environmental limitations to development were no more likely to occur within urbanized areas than at the urban fringe. Land in the western portion of Dade County is in the Everglades or in water conservation areas. In the exurban area just to the east of currently developed portions of King County, nine percent of the vacant acreage is either in wetlands or subject to slide hazards or subsidence. The same is true for 15 percent of the vacant acreage in the urbanized area.

---

6 City of Portland, *Vacant Lot Inventory*, p. 1.

In many areas, air pollution problems pose constraints for industrial infill development. Federal and state EPA regulations that limit the emission of additional pollutants from stationary sources in nonattainment areas could discourage industrial development on the relatively few sizable infill sites. Industries may well find that it is less costly to build outside of heavily urbanized areas.

Individual infill sites may have physical development limitations related to their shape or accessibility:

- Very long, narrow parcels (such as abandoned rights-of-way) will be usable only as trails or bicycle paths.
- Some sites will be undevelopable because they are located under or near electric transmission lines.
- Oddly shaped sites may be difficult to plan so as to conform to the setback and sideyard provisions of local zoning ordinances.
- Parcels lacking direct road frontage will require right-of-way acquisition and minor construction before they can be developed. This condition was observed for 15 percent of the sampled sites in King County, 12 percent in Monroe County, and five percent in Dade County.
- Development can also be constrained by severe soil problems, but this does not seem to be widespread. It affected eight percent of the suburban infill sites in Monroe County and four percent of the comparable sites in King County. In these cases, the soils would require extensive modification prior to development; the costs may be considered unacceptable under all but the most certain market conditions.

- In older urban areas, infilling often necessitates removal of buried foundations left over from earlier structures that were demolished. In cities where buildings are typically constructed with basements—as is common throughout the Northeast and Midwest—removal of subsurface materials can add considerably to site preparation costs. In examining five such sites in the city of Rochester, it is estimated that removing old foundations would add $691 to $3,404 to the per-unit construction costs of new townhouses, depending on the site.
- Where development is permitted in flood-prone areas, it may be necessary to provide fill (for low spots), as well as special drainage improvements and retention facilities. In Dade County, where soils are marshy and the terrain is flat, nearly two-thirds of the sampled infill parcels will require corrective action as a condition of development.

A very narrow bypassed parcel can present significant development problems. Some sites may be undevelopable because of the presence of electric transmission lines.

Seattle site with difficult terrain and an odd shape.

Codes and Review Procedures

A commonly cited obstacle to infilling is the perceived difficulty in meeting zoning, subdivision, and building standards in established communities. These problems are of three types:

- higher standards than in fringe areas
- lack of flexibility in dealing with site-specific problems
- high fees for building permits or utility connections.

For example, builders and developers interviewed by planning staff from the city of Omaha indicate that it is more difficult to build in the city than in outlying areas because the same standards are applied to one-of-a-kind infill situations as are required in new suburban fringe subdivisions. Developers may be asked to correct problems with existing infrastructure that originated many years ago. Knoxville planners point out that the city is far more restrictive in terms of what can be built in the floodplain or on hillsides than is Knox County. The city of San Diego has also recognized that development under its ordinances is more difficult and time consuming than in outlying parts of the region. In other instances, city standards may be the same as those in the outlying suburbs, but at the same time, they are inappropriate for high-density, pedestrian-oriented projects.

Ever-increasing standards have made it impossible to develop many smaller infill parcels without obtaining zoning variances. Lots with 30 feet of frontage often cannot be improved under current standards requiring 40-foot minimums. Mandating side yards of eight to 10 feet and setbacks of 20 feet or more results in the loss of much usable space on small lots and makes it difficult to exercise a site's full development potential. Obviously, some safeguards are necessary to assure that new infill development is compatible with nearby buildings from a design perspective. But in many areas, current site planning standards are more restrictive than those applying to surrounding older structures.

With respect to larger infill parcels, the problems may relate more to subdivision regulations than site or building standards. Commonly mentioned are street width requirements that add to on-site infrastructure costs and reduce net buildable areas; this is especially important at infill locations where land prices are high and developers need to make maximum use of the available land.

Property owners also voice some misgivings about the current zoning of their vacant land. Roughly 20 to 25 percent of the respondents with available properties in all three case studies suggest that a change in zoning would improve the marketability and development potential of their land. It is important to note, however, that such changes do not always involve a perceived need for higher densities. In the Rochester area, where the apartment market has been weak (and condominiums have yet to catch on), most of the complaints about current zoning come from owners of multifamily parcels rather than single-family parcels.

The ability of property owners to obtain zoning changes varies from city to city. Zoning decisions are becoming increasingly "political" rather than technical as neighborhood interests seek to modify (and sometimes stop) proposed zoning changes. At times, specific proposals are challenged because they are viewed as incompatible with existing uses or because of traffic or environmental problems they would generate. However, zoning changes may also be resisted in principle because neighbors fear that approving one change would open the door to many other less desirable requests.

Developers are under no legal obligation to meet with neighbors or to consult with zoning officials early in the development process, but it is prudent to do so to increase the likelihood of gaining needed approvals. In looking at as many as 50 buildings recently constructed on infill or redevelopment sites in each of the three case studies, RERC found that at least 20 percent of the builders/developers indicated that they consulted with neighborhood groups in advance of announcing their plans to the general public. This practice is likely to become more common in future years.

As important as the specific requirements of city regulations and codes is the way in which they are interpreted. When developers first approach city officials with a project, they want to know if it is worth pursuing or if it will be a frustrating waste of time. A clear understanding of the rules of the game and a sense that they will be administered fairly and consistently are as important as the stringency of the rules themselves. Although the property owners interviewed in the case studies could not all be expected to be familiar with city administrative procedures, a significant percentage indicated uncertainty about how local officials would respond to development proposals for their sites.

Availability of Financing

Infill development projects often involve "untested" locations and unusual building designs. Developers and builders point out that infilling is perceived to be risky and hence less attractive to lenders. However, conversations with both lenders and builders point to a developer's track record rather than location as the key factor influencing loan availability and terms for real estate projects. A builder with a proven record of successful projects will be viewed as a good risk. This can work against small-scale entrepreneurs who identify emerging opportunities for infilling but lack experience. These builders will have to use their own funds until they become established, or they will need to work initially with local governments and nonprofit local corporations with access to federal funds on a few demonstration projects, thereby proving their ability to manage and market new space successfully.

Infill and Suburban Fringe Housing: A Cost Comparison

Public officials and developers frequently have varying perceptions of the cost of infill housing as compared with urban fringe residential development. Public officials believe infill housing should be potentially less expensive for the consumer and local government because:

- The builder does not have to provide the expensive infrastructure required in fringe locations. Sewers, water lines, and roads are already in place for infill sites.
- Infill housing is less expensive for government to serve. The infrastructure has already been built and funds are already allocated for maintenance. Schools in infill neighborhoods generally have excess capacity. Wasteful duplication of facilities and services can be avoided.
- Residents of infill housing save money on transportation costs. They will drive shorter distances and own fewer cars because they have a public transportation option. They will be located closer to established shopping districts and recreation opportunities.

Developers, however, often hold conflicting beliefs regarding the costs associated with residential infill development. Generally, they consider infill development more expensive because:

- High land values in infill neighborhoods make market rate infill housing feasible only in the most affluent neighborhoods. Permitted densities in infill areas (especially suburban locations) are not high enough. Land costs cannot be spread over the number of units needed to lower unit costs and increase affordability.
- High land costs frequently consume savings from using existing infrastructure. Similarly, low land costs at the fringe enable developers to install new infrastructure and still provide middle-priced housing.
- Infill housing is more expensive to construct on a per-unit basis. The smaller number of units involved in a typical infill project precludes achieving scale economies obtainable on large fringe tracts.
- Living in infill housing is expensive. Higher taxes in infill neighborhoods—especially in central cities— may cause middle-income families to choose cheaper suburban locations.

Analyzing variations in costs of residential development borne by builders, consumers, and local governments helped clarify these conflicting beliefs. In each case study, three locations attractive for middle-priced, owner-occupied housing were identified—two infill areas (one in the central city, one in an established, "mature" suburb) and one area on the fringe of urban development. Within each of these areas, specific sites were selected for hypothetical construction of standard 1,500-square-foot attached townhouse units. RERC inspected each site, evaluated the infrastructure with local officials, and interviewed local developers and builders regarding construction costs. The cost to the builder of acquiring and developing the land, the cost to the consumer of purchasing and living in a unit, and the cost to local government of servicing the dend the cost to local government of servicing the development were estimated.

The Selection Process

The researchers looked for neighborhoods considered "typical" within the metropolitan area. Infill development areas had "normal" infrastructure conditions. Efforts were made to exclude areas with recently replaced utilities or with serious problems considered uncharacteristic of the system as a whole. Some sites within the infill areas did, however, need additional infrastructure work before they could be developed. The suburban infill development areas could be either incorporated or unincorporated as long as they were well established. Fringe areas were chosen that were presently rural in character, but in the path of future development activity.

To further assure comparability, the areas selected demonstrated "average" socioeconomic characteristics and had a market for middle-priced housing. Areas with luxury housing were excluded, as were neighborhoods where new residential construction would require subsidies.

Suburban townhouses in Reston, Virginia.

125

Site Selection

Within each infill development area, the researchers selected several development sites "typical" of the infill opportunities available.

Site selection was not restricted by the current zoning of the site—though an effort was made to select sites zoned for residential use. The required townhouse zoning was assumed to be obtainable for each site selected. All sites conformed to the minimum lot size requirements for townhouses. If 6,000 square feet was the minimum lot size on which townhouses were allowed, then all sites chosen contained at least 6,000 square feet. The applicable zoning regulations (side yard, setbacks, etc.) for townhouses were adhered to in each jurisdiction in determining the number of units that could be developed on each site.

The sites provided a representative range of physical development conditions and problems in the area. Sites with severe physical or environmental limitations were excluded, however. Generally, parcels at the urban fringe were not served by water and sewer to the property line. However, in the case of Monroe County, widespread extension of water lines along section line roads in advance of development made it impossible to find a suitable fringe area site that did not already have water service.

Standard Residential Unit

A constant housing type was used for all three study areas within each region to avoid variations in construction costs resulting from differences in unit size and design, rather than location. The standard unit chosen was a 1,500-square-foot, two-story attached townhouse with three bedrooms and two bathrooms. Modifications in style and building materials were made to correspond to local practice in each metropolitan area. The townhouse type was chosen based on the following rationale:

- Townhouses may be the most easily built form of infill housing that will be attractive to families. Single-family detached housing is often very costly to build on isolated city lots. Apartment buildings usually require more land assembly, face more local opposition, and are less attractive to families.
- Townhouses can be designed for larger fringe area tracts, as well as city lots.
- In many city and suburban locations, land costs are high. Townhouse construction lowers per-unit land costs so that new housing is more reasonable relative to prices of existing older houses.

The construction cost for these rowhouses in Portland, Oregon, was $38 per square foot of living area.

Estimating Costs to the Developer

For each of the sites chosen for hypothetical development, RERC estimated the developer's costs for acquiring and preparing the site, installing any needed on-site infrastructure, and erecting the townhouses. The items used to calculate the hypothetical development costs included:

Land. Estimated using common real estate appraisal techniques.

Off-site improvements. Included necessary road improvements and extension of public sewer, water, and other utility lines. In most cases, developers are required to bear these costs.

On-site improvements. Included all expenditures required for preparing the site. In addition to roads and utility lines, costs included those required to correct special drainage problems, landscaping, sewage holding tanks and pump stations, and for some infill sites, removal of existing foundations and debris. Both off-site and on-site improvement costs were estimated using regional cost calculators and information on local practices and conditions supplied by developers and public officials.

Construction. Calculated on a square foot basis for "good" quality materials and "good" quality design and construction. Although similar-sized townhouses are being built at both a greater and lesser cost in each metropolitan area, a middle-range cost was chosen—one which would provide a unit of reasonable quality that would be affordable to a broad segment of the market.

Fees and permits. For building permits, sewer hookups, platting fees, etc. These fees, while not adding considerably to the developer's costs, vary among jurisdictions.

Interim financing. Can vary considerably depending on the competence and experience of the builder in phasing the project and on changes in market forces that affect sellout time. Assuming a market in all locations, financing costs were held constant in each case study. In determining constant financing costs, several calculations were made using different assumptions on phasing and sellout periods. A "typical" per-unit financing cost was then selected for use in determining the probable unit selling price.

Overhead. "Soft costs" (architectural, engineering, legal fees, and marketing expenses) for the hypothetical developments, figured as percentages of hard costs (construction, site preparation, off-site improvements, etc.). Percentages were based on local practice and custom in each county as determined through interviews with builders and developers. They were held constant throughout a metropolitan area unless a consistent variation within the region could be demonstrated.

Profit. Calculated as a percentage of the total project cost. If local developers consistently try to make a 25 percent pretax profit on a project, then a 25 percent profit margin was included in the calculations to determine the selling price of a unit. Developers frequently do not make the profit they aspire to, especially if they happen to be the first to build infill housing in a neighborhood.

Calculating Consumer Costs

The researchers estimated the cost of purchasing and living in an infill townhouse in the city or a mature suburb compared with purchasing and living in a similar unit at the urban fringe. Expenditures for an identical unit can vary considerably because of home heating or electricity use (which can vary depending on how many people are at home during an average day) or maintenance (some households spend more than others), for example. Fringe areas usually have a larger number of persons per household than inner city areas. For this analysis, however, household size was assumed constant for all locations (three persons per household was used to estimate transportation costs). Averages for each area were used to calculate costs. The elements considered in these calculations included: mortgage financing, homeowners insurance, property taxes and user fees, maintenance costs, and transportation costs (auto and transit).

Calculating Local Government Costs

Three major categories of servicing costs for local government were investigated and calculated. Costs were estimated for:

Schools. Interviews were conducted with local school officials to determine how much new development could occur before additional school space would be required. In areas where there was excess school capacity, the new residential development would result in little or no increased cost for the school system. School officials considered the administrative costs involved in redistricting or rerouting some bus lines to be negligible.

For areas where new schools would be required, researchers used the average per pupil cost of constructing new facilities within the local school district. Per pupil operating costs were obtained through interviews with local school officials.

Roads. Estimates were made only for roads constructed or improved by local government. Although the costs of building streets within the development site are normally borne by the developer, the increased traffic caused by new houses could necessitate improvements to existing off-site streets and roads, the cost of which would be borne by the community. In addition, any on-site streets for which the local government accepts dedication will require public expenditures for maintenance. Costs for constructing or improving existing roads were estimated using cost calculators and estimates of local officials. Few communities, however, have figures on per mile maintenance costs, so it is difficult to estimate the marginal costs associated with maintaining new roads. The possible dedications were so small for the subject sites that it was assumed that the marginal maintenance cost to local government would be negligible. In the aggregate, however, extensive suburban fringe development causes greater maintenance burdens, while infill housing shares the cost of existing maintenance among a larger number of taxpayers, therefore lowering the cost to each.

Sewer and Water. Most local governments require that any extension of water or sewer lines to a new development site be paid for by the developer. If, however, existing lines are operating at capacity, enlarging those lines would require public expenditures. Similarly, the cost for expanding sewer or water treatment capacity would be borne by the local government. Capital costs for increasing sewer and water capacities or repairing the existing infrastructure were estimated using cost calculators and estimates of local officials. With respect to ongoing line maintenance, the situation is similar to that described for roads. An individual development project of 200 units at the fringe does not result in significant maintenance outlays. Yet if all similarly sized tracts were so developed, the requirements would be extensive.

Several perceptions about the cost of infill development appeared to be valid:

- Per-unit costs for infrastructure and site development were higher on the fringe than in infill areas.
- Land was less expensive on the fringe than in infill areas.
- Transportation costs were higher on the fringe than in infill areas.

But overall, infilling did not result in substantial private cost savings when compared to fringe development. Major savings in one cost category were offset by higher costs in another. Public cost savings from infilling were evident primarily through reduction in maintenance obligations for new roads and utilities.

It is very difficult, however, to generalize about the costs of infill versus fringe area development. Within each metropolitan region, many factors affect the cost of infill development (varying from neighborhood to neighborhood). Unique circumstances in each case study affected costs for either the developer, consumer, or local government.

Cost to the Developer

For each of the sites chosen for analysis, the researchers estimated the developer's cost for acquiring and preparing the site, installing any needed on-site or off-site infrastructure, and erecting the standard townhouses. Variables that were not influenced by location were held constant (either in absolute terms or as a percentage of other costs) when determining an eventual selling price.

Dade County, with its booming residential market, showed an average estimated selling price of approximately $96,000 per unit. In Monroe County, where the market has been stagnant, the average price would be $75,000. In King County, the average price would be around $86,000—though there was a considerably greater variation in prices among locations in King County than in the other two counties. Figure 6-1 presents the weighted average selling prices for units in all three areas of each case study county.

The variation in prices among the metropolitan areas resulted primarily from differences in land values. The land values themselves reflected the relative strengths of residential markets in the three areas.

Land Prices

The main variable, both among the three counties and among fringe and infill areas within counties, was the price of land. Infill land was, on the average, almost 15 times more expensive per acre in Monroe County, but only four times as expensive in King County and less than twice as expensive in Dade County. Exurban land prices in Monroe County were relatively low; supplies were ample and demand was weak. The opposite was true in Dade County, where high growth rates stimulate demand for raw land and growth controls and environmental limitations constrain supply. Price variations are shown in Figure 6-2, along with the value of the land as a percentage of the selling price. Raw land in Dade County accounted for between 10 and 16 percent of the selling price of a townhouse unit. These percentages were based on the price of land as if it were already zoned for townhouse development. Land prices in Dade County were especially sensitive to zoning. An acre of land on the fringe selling for $36,000 without zoning would sell for at least $80,000 with townhouse zoning in place.

In both Monroe and King Counties, the percentage of the purchase price attributable to land value was greater in the mature suburb than in the central city. In Monroe County, both the greater densities allowed in the city and the comparable land values in the mature suburb contributed to this effect. In King County, per unit land price variations between the inner city and mature suburb were

---

Figure 6-1
Townhouse Selling Prices
(Weighted Averages)

	Miami (Dade County)	Seattle (King County)	Rochester (Monroe County)
Inner City	$97,931 (88/26)*	$80,042 (106/11)	$74,896 (114/9)
Mature Suburb	$95,854 (153/5)	$91,299 (139/5)	$75,537 (201/4)
Urban Fringe	$94,889 (200/1)	$85,797 (200/1)	$75,171 (200/1)

*Figures in parentheses indicate the number of dwelling units and sites examined in each location.

Figure 6-2
Land Cost Comparisons
(Weighted Averages)

	Miami (Dade County)	Seattle (King County)	Rochester (Monroe County)
Inner City			
Per square foot	$ 6.46	$ 2.36	$ .50
Per acre	$281,078	$101,783	$21,725
Per unit[1]	$ 15,691	$ 4,319	$ 1,311
Number of units/acre[2]	18	24	16
Raw land as percent of selling price	16.02	5.26	1.75
Mature Suburb			
Per square foot	$ 2.60	$ .93	$ .51
Per acre	$113,259	$ 40,301	$22,101
Per unit[1]	$ 13,484	$ 7,472	$ 1,855
Number of units/acre	8.5	5.5	12
Raw land as percent of selling price	14.07	8.18	2.46
Urban Fringe			
Per square foot	$ 1.84	$ .28	$ .03
Per acre	$ 80,000	$ 12,000	$ 1,500
Per unit[1]	$ 9,412	$ 2,182	$ 150
Number of units/acre	8.5	5.5	12
Raw land as percent of selling price	9.92	2.54	0.20

[1]Based on densities actually achievable under townhouse zoning regulations. If the same densities could be achieved at the suburban and fringe sites as in the central cities, per unit land costs in the cities would appear even less favorable by comparison.

[2]Miami and Rochester permit up to 24 units/acre, but setback, sideyard, and other requirements limited actual densities to an average of 18 and 16 units per acre respectively.

strictly a function of the greater densities achievable in the city—24.2 dwelling units per acre compared with 5.5 dwelling units per acre in the suburban area.

Higher densities could have been achieved on some sites in both the mature and fringe suburbs of Dade and King Counties by using planned unit development (PUD) rather than townhouse zoning. This would have lowered the per-unit land costs and made the price of housing in both the mature suburban and fringe areas more attractive in comparison to central city housing.

Infrastructure and Site Development Costs

The costs of preparing the site and providing the infrastructure for townhouse developments were, on the average, higher per unit on the fringe than for the infill areas. Fringe area site improvement costs averaged at least $1,000 more per unit than in infill locations in all three counties. This cost difference was, however, more than offset by the higher cost of land in the infill areas. The site improvement and infrastructure costs are summarized in Figure 6-3.

The supposed advantages of infill sites in keeping site development costs down were evident only in Seattle, where maximum use could be made of the existing infrastructure. In both Seattle and Rochester, however, the cost of removing buried foundations from previously developed sites added as much as $3,000 per unit to the development costs for certain vacant parcels analyzed. In Rochester, larger parcels required considerable on-site infrastructure. In one instance, a new sewer line was required for a currently unserviced street. In Miami, the zoning ordinance required that automobiles be able to turn around on the site. Parking spaces had to be provided underneath the dwelling units. This required additional grading and the construction of retaining walls, which considerably increased site development costs. The most extensive off-site costs in an infill area occurred in the mature suburban area of Dade County.

Because much of the county is developed on septic fields, many built-up areas do not have sewers. While the land could be used for single-family homes with on-site disposal systems, townhouse densities would require additional infrastructure.

Figure 6-3
Infrastructure and Site Development
Cost Comparisons
(Per-Unit Weighted Averages)[1]

	Miami (Dade County)	Seattle (King County)	Rochester (Monroe County)
Inner City			
On-Site[2]	$3,069	$1,057	$1,703
Off-Site[3]	0	0	252
Total	$3,069	$1,057	$1,955
Mature Suburb			
On-Site[2]	$1,836	$1,434	$1,469
Off-Site[3]	714	390	0
Total	$2,550	$2,824	$1,469
Urban Fringe			
On-Site[2]	$2,912	$1,065	$1,407
Off-Site[3]	1,218	1,427	1,305
Total	$4,130	$3,492	$2,712

[1]Based on densities permitted under existing townhouse zoning provisions.
[2]Includes costs for all on-site sewer and water lines, access streets, and drives.
[3]Includes costs of extending sewer and water lines to the site. In the King County mature suburb, included frontage-foot assessment for sewer and water already in place.

Construction Costs, Fees, and Financing Charges

Construction costs varied slightly among the three metropolitan regions. Per square foot costs in Dade County were $31 compared with $32.50 in Monroe County and $33.17 in King County. No variation could be documented, however, between infill and fringe locations within each metropolitan area. Building permits and other fees varied among political jurisdictions. Valid generalizations could not be made regarding higher costs for infill versus fringe projects. In Rochester and Seattle, fees were lower in the central city than in the suburban and fringe areas. In Miami, fees were slightly higher in the city than for areas in unincorporated Dade County. The largest variation among any of the jurisdictions was in Seattle, where the per-unit fees in the mature suburban area were $752 higher than in the city.

Financing practices were the same in all three metropolitan areas, and the terms were held constant for all of the comparisons.

Builders generally estimate overhead expenses as a percent of total project costs. Stringent environmental impact assessment requirements in Dade and King Counties made per unit overhead costs slightly higher than in Monroe County.

Perceptions concerning the inability to achieve economies of scale on small infill parcels could neither be verified nor disproved. Scale economies were heavily influenced by the size (and thus the overhead), experience, and competence of individual development firms and could not be related to the location and size of the building sites alone.

Consumer Costs

The major consumer cost variable between infill and fringe area locations was transportation. Persons living on the fringe had to drive farther, on the average, to get to work, shopping, and recreation. Persons living in the inner city usually had a public transportation alternative to driving. They frequently could make shopping and other trips on foot.

The transportation cost differential was greatest in Dade County. Employment and shopping opportunities were available within walking distance of the inner city neighborhood in Miami. In contrast, the Seattle city neighborhood had fewer walking opportunities; inner city residents tended to make just as many automobile trips per capita as residents of the fringe area. However, the steep terrain and limited number of bridges across Seattle area lakes create circuitous routes that resulted in longer average trip lengths for fringe area residents. Thus, the transportation cost differential between the inner city and fringe areas is still almost $4,000 in King County.

Although taxes and other charges were higher in each central city than at the fringe, the greatest difference was $850 in Dade County. In Monroe and King Counties, the difference was only $200 to $300. King County was the only case where utility costs varied by location. Seattle has municipal electric service, while the mature suburban and fringe areas are served by a private utility company. As a result, average electric charges in Seattle were estimated at about $120 per unit less than those in the other two areas.

Costs to Local Government

None of the hypothetical developments analyzed in this research was large enough by itself to force public capital expenditures for schools, roads, or utilities. Yet the cumulative effect of several developments would require public capital outlay for a number of the areas studied. For instance, the sewer line that would have to be extended in order to serve the fringe area in Monroe County was approaching capacity and could take only about 100 more connections. The 200-unit development postulated for this study required extending lines a few hundred feet farther in the opposite direction to tap into another line. A similar situation existed in the mature suburban area in Dade County.

Contrary to common beliefs, some fringe area schools were not overcrowded and certain infill area schools did not have excess capacity. In Dade and King Counties, the cumulative effect of new fringe development would result in overcrowding and construction of new schools. In Monroe County, however, the fringe area school district had excess capacity.

The mature suburban school districts had excess capacity in all three counties, and the city of Rochester's schools also had room for additional students. However, in Seattle and Miami, schools in the central city infill neighborhoods were crowded.

In Miami, this crowding resulted from the recent closing of an obsolete building and an influx of new immigrants from Cuba and South America. In Seattle, a school integration program that pairs schools in different ethnic neighborhoods caused overcrowding in individual buildings, even though the city as a whole had excess capacity.

With respect to utilities and roads, the quantity of infill or fringe area development analyzed would not directly generate new capital costs for local government. The capital costs for both on- and off-site infrastructure would be borne by the developers. The addition of new streets, sewers, and water lines generated by the hypothetical projects, however, would require local government exenditures for maintenance. It is extremely difficult to estimate the marginal maintenance costs associated with this new infrastructure. Figure 6-4 summarizes the number of linear feet of sewer and water lines and the number of square yards of new street surface that would have to be maintained by local governmental units in each location.

Figure 6-4
Potential Government Service Burden Comparisons

	Miami (Dade County)	Seattle (King County)	Rochester (Monroe County)
Inner City			
Utilities (average linear ft./unit)[1]	None	6 ft.	51 ft.
Streets (average sq. yds./unit)[2]	None	None	30 sq. yds.
Schools[3]	Jr. high crowded	Schools crowded	None
Mature Suburb			
Utilities[1]	98 ft. (plus lift station)	78 ft.	87 ft.
Streets[2]	70 sq. yds.	87 sq. yds.	35 sq. yds.
Schools[3]	None	None	None
Urban Fringe			
Utilities[1]	176 feet (plus lift station)	154 feet (plus lift station)	113 feet (plus storage pond and pump)
Streets[2]	79.5 sq. yds.	88 sq. yds.	21 sq. yds.
Schools[3]	Jr. high crowding critical	New schools totaling $28 million opening 1980 and 1981	None

[1]Local government would not incur capital costs for utilities in any of the hypothesized developments. The utility extensions to the sites and some on-site lines however, would become the responsibility of local government for maintenance and repair.
[2]For streets, as for utilities, all capital costs would be absorbed by the developers, but new on-site access streets would frequently be dedicated to local government for maintenance and repair.
[3]Incremental development eventually requires capital expenditures for new schools. None of the hypothesized developments, however, would be large enough by itself to justify a new school.

Conclusions

From the consumer's perspective, purchasing and living in a townhouse built on a central city infill site appears to be less costly than living in a similar unit on the fringe of urban development. However, household life-styles can affect the cost equation significantly. Families with children who prefer city living may feel a need to incur private school tuition charges; other child-oriented households will choose suburban locations even if they are more expensive. Higher taxes and other costs in the city will likely be more than offset by the greater transportation costs associated with living on the fringe. In those situations where land prices and site develop-ment costs make the central city infill sites less expensive to develop, the savings to the consumer would be even greater. But because tax levels and commuting patterns vary among metropolitan areas and are constantly changing, these conclusions must be viewed cautiously.

The cost advantages of infill from the perspectives of developers and local government are even less certain. Developers' costs are influenced by site characteristics, neighborhood conditions, governmental regulations, and the size and structure of the developers' organization. In some situations, the same unit can be produced for less on an infill site than on a fringe area site. In other cases, it will cost more to develop infill sites. Similarly, fringe area development generally increases costs of local government by generating a need for more schools and increasing the amount of infrastructure to be maintained. Yet some local governments have overbuilt their facilities to the point that additional development actually lowers the per-unit cost of operating and maintaining those facilities.

The ability of infill development to reduce housing costs depends very much on local conditions. Even from the consumer's perspective, the cost savings for transpor-tation associated with living on infill sites may not be great enough to overcome perceived intangible benefits derived from living on the urban fringe. The lifestyles and housing preferences of individual consumers will be as important as cost considerations in making locational choices.

DATE DUE		